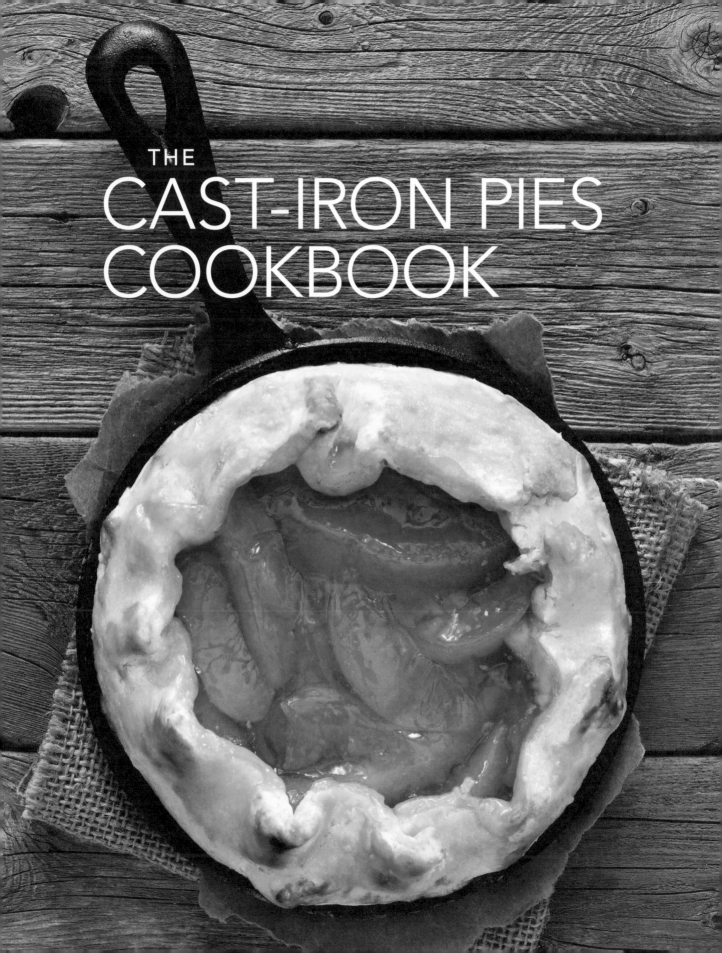

THE
CAST-IRON PIES
COOKBOOK

THE
CAST-IRON PIES
COOKBOOK

101 Delicious Pie Recipes
for Your Cast-Iron Cookware

Dominique DeVito

CIDER MILL PRESS

BOOK PUBLISHERS

Kennebunkport, Maine

13-Digit ISBN: 9781604336955
10-Digit ISBN: 1604336951

This book may be ordered by mail from the publisher. Please include $5.99 for postage and handling.
Please support your local bookseller first!

Books published by Cider Mill Press Book Publishers are available at special discounts for bulk purchases in the United States by corporations, institutions, and other organizations. For more information, please contact the publisher.

Cider Mill Press Book Publishers
"Where good books are ready for press"
PO Box 454
12 Spring Street
Kennebunkport, Maine 04046

Visit us on the Web! www.cidermillpress.com

Cover design by Alicia Freile, Tango Media
Interior design by Alicia Freile, Tango Media
Typography: Avenir, Fairfield, Fenway Park, Gotham, Journal, Linotype Centennial, Minion, Neo Retro Draw, Neo Retro Fill, and Influence Medium

Image Credits: Page 78 © StockFood / Keller & Keller Photography; Page 81 © StockFood / Norwood Browne, Angie; Page 82 © StockFood / Hwang, Kent; Page 109 © StockFood / Bill, Arce; Page 111 © StockFood / Hoff, Dana; Page 119 © StockFood / Bill Milne Studio; Page 125 © StockFood / Leatart, Brian; Page 126 © StockFood / Short, Jonathan; Page 195 © StockFood / Richard Jackson Photography; Page 231 © StockFood / Robbins, Heath; All other images used under official license from Shutterstock.com

Printed in China

1 2 3 4 5 6 7 8 9 0
First Edition

CONTENTS

WHY CAST-IRON IS HERE TO STAY

There's nothing particularly attractive about a cast-iron skillet on the outside. It's all black, no shiny chrome, no flashy stainless steel, and it's heavy. And the handles get hot. And if the pan hasn't been properly cared for, it can get rusty or look grungy, which is how many of them end up at flea markets, where the dust really shows on them because they're…black.

But boy-oh-boy is there something attractive about a cast-iron skillet that's in good shape and properly cared for. In sum, it is one of the best cooking tools you can have.

AND HERE'S WHY:

Cast-iron gets hot and distributes and holds heat like no other pan, which gives you a greater range of temperatures to work with. For example, if you're sautéing onions in a stainless-steel skillet, it gets hot quickly, and it also loses its heat exponentially when it is removed from it or the heat is lowered. Sautéed onions are best when cooked slowly and evenly so they caramelize without burning. When your cast-iron skillet is good and hot and you've started the process,

you can lower the heat and know that the temperature won't fall off so much that you have to play with it as you continue to cook. And that's just one example.

Cast-iron skillets can go directly from the stove to the oven, and from the oven to the table, saving a lot of additional dishes for serving and a lot of time at clean-up. Yes, the handles get hot, but they're an extension of the skillets themselves and so will never melt or fall off.

Another great thing about the cast-iron is the material itself—iron. Women, especially, tend to be diagnosed with iron deficiencies in their modern-day diets. Beneficial iron leaches into foods cooked in the cast-iron skillet. It won't compensate for iron deficiency, but it's helpful—and certainly better than the chemicals leaching from "nonstick" coatings, which have been shown to contribute to liver damage, developmental problems, cancer, and early menopause.

If you aren't sold yet, there's the durability of cast-iron. These skillets are family heirlooms; they last as long as they're maintained properly. In fact, there's something wonderful about a cast-iron skillet that's been passed down from mother to daughter, father to son, grandparent to grandchild. There are stories in your family's cast-iron skillets, and there are stories you'll be telling about yours.

THE HISTORY OF CAST-IRON COOKWARE

Cast-iron is the product of pouring molten iron into a mold, letting it cool, and then refining it for its purpose (whether it be a pot, a bench, a piece of equipment, etc.). The Chinese were the first to develop foundries that could manage this, and it's estimated to date back several hundred years BC. Here in the West, iron foundries are estimated to date back to the 11th century. Large cauldrons were some of the first cooking implements to come out of the foundries, and they were prized for being able to hold a lot, maintain temperatures, and sit solidly over a fire. Just as in ancient China, the process of making cast-iron pieces in the West involved pouring the hot metal into a mold made from sand and, when cast, removing the sand mold and grinding the piece to smooth its surfaces.

Fast-forward to our European ancestors in the mid-19th century, where cooking was done in hearths. The cookware was adapted so that pieces could be moved or repositioned more easily, and cast-iron cauldrons were built with longer handles and legs. Dutch ovens—compact cookware closely resembling what we call Dutch ovens today—were forged to be placed directly on coals. As the oven itself evolved, the flat cast-iron skillet was created for use on an open "burner" or to be placed in the closed part of the cook stove.

AN AMERICAN EVOLUTION

Here in America, the first cast-iron foundry was established in 1619. Early settlers to the United States brought cookware with them, of course, and fashioned their hearths in the styles of what they were used to in their homelands. Cooking continued to be done in fireplaces or over open fires until modern plumbing made it possible to access water from faucets in the home. Cooks rejoiced, and running water became part of a true kitchen. Wood and coal fueled the fires that enabled cooking and heating of homes until gas companies developed ways to make ovens fueled by gas in the 1900s. It didn't take too much longer for electric ovens to come onto the scene—in the 1930s—though they didn't become really popular until the price of electricity fell, in the 1960s. Through all these developments, cast-iron remained the cookware of choice because it was still the most durable and practical.

It wasn't until after World War II—in the late 1940s/early 1950s—that stainless steel and aluminum emerged as materials for pots and pans. The factories that had been making guns and tanks had a lot of it, and the fact that these metals were lighter in weight than cast-iron and didn't rust made them highly desirable by homemakers. In quick succession all manner of pots and pans were formed with these metals, and a nonstick coating was developed to make their care even easier. Teflon was approved by the US Food and Drug Administration in 1960, and its popularity took off, pushing cast-iron to the back of the cabinet.

THE RESURGENCE OF ITS USE AND POPULARITY

It seems cooks started dragging the cast-iron skillets out from the backs of their pantries in earnest again by the late 2000s. The trend was confirmed when the *LA Times* published an article in November 2012 declaring, "Cast-iron enjoys a comeback among cooks." The author, Noelle Carter, attributed part of the resurgence to the fact that the company making the cookware—Lodge Manufacturing—had introduced pre-seasoned cast-iron. According to Lodge, this was an industry first that has now become an industry standard, as it eliminates having to continually season the cookware.

For me, personally, I have skillets and Dutch ovens that I've inherited, and some that I've purchased. Being careful to care for the cookware (as detailed in the next chapter), I have found it to always live up to my expectations. My cast-iron cookware heats beautifully and without smoking even without the addition of oil or fat in the skillet; the things I cook in it come out without sticking to the surface; it's a joy to be able to start something on the stove and then finish it in the oven; they seem to get better and better with use (which is not true of Teflon-coated pans); and maybe best of all, my kids have taken to using them and discovering their simplicity and practicality (though I have to remind them about not using soap to clean them).

When the assignment came to write a book focused on baking in cast-iron, I was worried that I couldn't come up with enough recipes. Turns out, as usual, that a cook is really only limited by his or her time and imagination. When I realized I could make any number of variations to boxed cake mixes, my family almost got sick of the variations I came up with. After the initial worry about heating up the lid of the Dutch oven in the bread-making process (I was concerned about melting in the high heat, which didn't happen), I learned that there is nothing yummier than a loaf cooked in a cast-iron Dutch oven. The crust is always great, and the inside airy and light.

WHICH PIECES FOR WHICH DISHES?

Now that cast-iron is popular again, you can find skillets and other pieces in a range of sizes. If you do an online search for cast-iron cookware, you'll find two names that come up a lot: Lodge and Williams-Sonoma. Lodge is a manufacturer (see sidebar), and you can buy pieces directly from them, or from retailers that sell their products. A manufacturer of enamel-coated cast-iron is the French company, Le Creuset. Williams-Sonoma sells it in many colors and sizes, and it's beautiful (if heavy). As with most things, you'll get what you pay for with your

cast-iron, too. A simple skillet may look pricey compared to stainless steel or Teflon, but considering you'll be using it almost daily for decades and it'll just be getting better, it's a necessary investment. Lodge and Le Creuset are manufacturers you can completely trust.

Lodge makes skillets ranging from 3.5 inches in diameter up to 13.25 inches in diameter. They also make deep skillets, griddles (and covers), Dutch ovens, and specialized bakeware like cornstick pans and mini cake pans.

You are welcome to experiment with any of the sizes, but here's great news: For all the recipes in this book, I used a 12 inch skillet.

Seasoning Vs. Pre-Seasoned

The concept of seasoning a cast-iron skillet or other piece of cookware is to protect it from rusting and to aid in proper cooking. Part of the reason cast-iron fell out of favor with home cooks was that keeping the cookware properly seasoned was an essential chore. When Lodge introduced pre-seasoned cast-iron in the early 2000s, keeping the cookware seasoned became a whole lot easier. The cookware now has a nice sheen and surface that ensures great results right from the start. The seasoning process Lodge does to its cookware uses vegetable oil, just as cooks were instructed to do when seasoning their unseasoned cookware for the first time. And it doesn't hurt a pre-seasoned piece to get "re-seasoned" using the process outlined in the next section.

The important thing is the maintenance of the cookware. When it is washed (without soap), dried thoroughly (including the bottom, sides, and handles), and rubbed with enough vegetable oil to give it a smooth shine without appearing oily, then the cookware is ready for its next assignment.

Lodge Manufacturing

The history of the oldest US manufacturer of cast-iron cookware is impressive. It all started when Joseph Lodge settled with his family in South Pittsburgh, Tennessee in the late 1800s. Lodge opened the Blacklock Foundry there in 1896, named after a minister who was a friend. A fire struck in 1910, and the foundry was rebuilt just blocks from its original location. It was renamed the Lodge Manufacturing Company.

Next came two World Wars and the Great Depression. The factory managed to survive by casting decorative pieces for a richer clientele until it could get back to focusing on cookware. The family persisted in modernizing its facility. Two neighboring foundries closed by the 1940s. Business wasn't booming for Lodge after that, either, but it survived because of the quality and durability of the product and the efficiency with which its products were—and continue to be—made. The breakthrough for the company was the introduction of pre-seasoned pieces, which took the confusion out of prepping the cookware for use. Another reason cast-iron made a comeback is because the seasoning is non-toxic (vegetable oil)—which became important when Teflon's role in health problems started to be questioned. And of course, the cookware will have a very long lifetime.

Today, the factory is thriving in the otherwise sleepy town of South Pittsburg, Tennessee, whose population hovers at about 3,300. Nearly everyone knows someone who works for Lodge. A 2014 report in Bloomberg Business said, "According to the Cookware Manufacturers Association, shipments of cast-iron and similar enameled products in the U.S. have increased more than 225 percent since 2003—rising from $35 million to more than $114 million—while shipments of cookware in general increased by just a third." That's good news for Lodge, which celebrates its 120th anniversary this year (2016). The challenge now becomes how to maintain the popularity of something, that, with proper care, you don't really need to buy another of for about 100 years. Last but not least, if you're ever in South Pittsburg, you can visit the Lodge Factory Store, where over 2000 products are sold, and if you go in late April, you might catch the National Cornbread Festival (www.nationalcornbread.com). Thank you, Lodge!

THE CARE & KEEPING OF YOUR CAST-IRON COOKWARE

We cooks have so many options when it comes to preparing foods: ovens, stoves, microwaves, grills, stainless steel, crockery, electric slow cookers, and woks. Among all these choices, a very old cooking tool—cast-iron is experiencing a renaissance of sorts in the modern kitchen. When you season and prep cast-iron and start using it to make the delectable selection of recipes in this cookbook, you'll soon discover why it has stood the test of time—and is redefining the modern family's practices.

You may already be familiar with a cast-iron skillet. It's the plain, black, one-piece pan that always seemed to be at the back of the stack of fry pans in the cupboard. If you can remember where you saw that old pan, by all means, go get it. Acquiring a piece of cast-iron cookware from someone in your family is a way of keeping history alive. You'll be carrying on a tradition of cooking and serving foods that has been passed through generations. If, on the other hand, you're new to using cast-iron and you are the one to acquire it in your family, you can look forward to sharing its results with your family and to someday passing it on to your children or grandchildren.

Besides being an amazing piece of cookware, cast-iron does, indeed, last a lifetime (or more)—so long as it's properly cared for. It's simple enough to do, but it's important to do it properly, not only before you use a pan for the first time but before and after every use. Here's how it is done.

SEASONING A NEW SKILLET

When I went shopping for a new cast-iron skillet, I came upon Lodge pans—a company that has been making cast-iron skillets since the late 1800s. They brand themselves as "America's Original Cookware." Since nothing stands completely still, they have recently developed a method to season their cookware so that it will last as it always has but with minimal (consistent) care. That's a good thing! What they do is coat the pan with vegetable oil and bake it in at very high heat, which is just what you need to do to an unseasoned pan. With a new Lodge seasoned piece, you can be cooking from it almost immediately.

But let's start at the beginning, with an unseasoned skillet. Here's the procedure to bring it into use:

1. Wash with hot, soapy water.

2. Rinse and dry thoroughly.

3. If there's any rust on the pan, sand it lightly with fine-grained sandpaper. Apply Coca-Cola to the rust spots and leave on for 10 to 15 minutes. Wash again with soapy water, rinse, dry and put the skillet on a burner over low heat to dry any excess moisture.

4. If there's no rust, after drying the cookware all over, apply a light layer of cooking oil (vegetable oil, NOT olive oil, butter, or margarine!) all over the pan with a paper towel, rubbing even the handle. The pan should have a light sheen to it.

5. Place the skillet upside down on the middle rack of the oven and preheat the oven to 400 degrees. Put a piece of foil or a baking dish on the lower rack to catch any drips of oil. Let the pan cook in the oven for about 2 hours.

6. Turn the oven off and let the pan cool (upside down) in the oven.

7. Take it out, wipe it down with a clean paper towel, and it's good to go.

8. If your pan has taken on a slightly brown color, you can repeat the process, which will further season the pan and darken its color, improving its appearance. This will also happen over time.

CARING FOR YOUR CAST-IRON

Rule #1: Never wash your seasoned pan with soapy water!
Rule #2: Never put a cast-iron pan in the dishwasher!

Why? Soap breaks down the protective seasoning, and you have to re-season the pan all over again. Leaving any kind of water on the pan will lead to rusting, which will demand re-seasoning from the beginning. It seems counter-intuitive, especially when you're used to thinking "it's not clean unless it's been washed in (really) hot, soapy water," but it's actually a great thing about cast-iron.

After you've cooked in your skillet, clean it with hot water (no soap) and a plastic, rough-surfaced scrub brush. Dry the cookware completely (all over) after washing. Put a teaspoon of vegetable oil in the pan and, with a paper towel, rub it in all over the pan until it has a nice sheen. Take a fresh paper towel and wipe the cookware dry. Store it where there is good air circulation so no moisture is trapped on it. If you need to stack it, put paper towels on the top and bottom.

GIVE IT A LOT OF LOVE

The best thing to do with your cast-iron skillet is USE IT! When you start using it for all the different things it can do (as evidenced by the diversity of recipes in this book), you'll probably find that the skillet lives on your stovetop, waiting for its next assignment. The more you use it, the better it gets. Nothing will stick to its surface. You can go from the frying pan to the fire, as it were, starting a dish on the stove and finishing it in the oven. You can cook your skillet to a very high heat (or put it in the campfire), and it'll cook up the food you put in it beautifully (so long as you keep an eye on it).

In short, with regular use, the cast-iron skillet truly is a pan that will just keep cooking and cooking, getting better and better with age and use. Just like you and me!

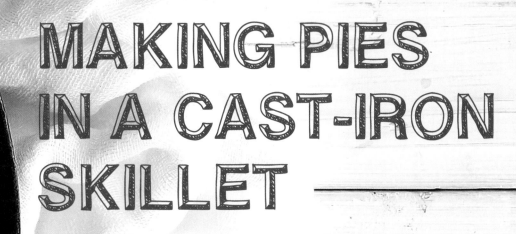

MAKING PIES IN A CAST-IRON SKILLET

The thing I've learned about cast-iron skillets is that, once you start using them regularly, they truly become your go-to cooking instruments. They're so versatile and so easy to use. They conduct heat beautifully, and the fact that they can go from stovetop to oven is a real bonus.

Using a cast-iron skillet to bake a pie? That seemed a stretch at first. After all, there are oodles of pie plates specifically designed for pies, in every kind of material and with different decorations and trims. Why go for basic cast-iron? Here's why: Flavor. And, yes, the overall look of the pie in the cast-iron. There's something very elemental about it.

This book has recipes for making all kinds of pies in a cast-iron skillet, from traditional fruit pies with fancy top crusts to simple folded-crust galettes to savory casserole-type "shepherd's" pies and of course a variety of quiches. There are recipes for different kinds of crusts, too – everything from the basic crust to a gluten-free option to crusts you can fashion from cookies or nuts. Deliciousness abounds!

The most important part of making a pie in a cast-iron skillet is fitting the crust in the skillet. You'll see that the crust recipes call for melting butter in the skillet before placing the crust in it. That's to help with keeping the crust from sticking to the bottom of the skillet. The more seasoned your skillet the more successful your pie, as there is little that will stick to a well-seasoned skillet. If your skillet isn't so seasoned, you may want to increase the amount of butter you melt in it before placing and pressing the crust into the pan. One benefit of doing this is that every pie contributes to seasoning the skillet.

Another thing to be aware of is overall cooking time. Because a cast-iron skillet is such a good conductor of heat, cooking times can vary. The recipes indicate active and overall times for the recipes, but they assume that the crust is already prepared. If you've made a crust ahead of time and have kept the skillet in the refrigerator until you're ready to fill and bake it, you'll need to factor in additional cooking time as the skillet will be cold going into the oven.

I like to keep things simple in my kitchen, so I tend to use the same skillet for everything. It's a Lodge 12-inch skillet and it's a fabulous pan. I have a very good sense of how thin to roll out my crusts so they work in the skillet. You'll get the hang of that, too. I prefer to make a standard-sized pie even if it's only me who'll be eating it, because I can refrigerate the rest and have leftovers. That's rare, though, because I have kids (and their friends) who are always on the lookout for what I've been baking. If I made a single-serving pie I'd have to hide to eat it! If you'd prefer to use a small skillet and make a pie for one or two people, that's absolutely possible. Make the crust per the directions and just put half the dough in the refrigerator for use later in the week (keep it wrapped tightly in plastic wrap).

Baking can seem intimidating, and I certainly felt that way when I was starting out. When you're making things like souffles or cakes or even bread – things that need to rise – it's especially important to heed the directions for quantities of ingredients. Pies, I'm happy to say, are more forgiving. And honestly, if you don't want to make a basic crust from scratch, there are very tasty alternatives, including the wrapped crusts you can find in the frozen foods section of the grocery store, and the box mixes that just need to have water added before being rolled out.

Don't psych yourself out into thinking you're entering a pie-baking competition with every one that you make. Toss some fruit with some sugar and spices, lay it on the crust, and see what happens. Line a crust with cheese and steamed veggies and bacon bits if you want, pour beaten eggs over it, and bake. Don't overcomplicate things. Your skillet – and your family – will accept your best intentions and be thankful for them.

No one said it better than the playwright David Mamet in Boston Marriage: "We must have a pie. Stress cannot exist in the presence of a pie."

PIE CRUST RECIPES

When most of us think of a pie, we think of a traditional flour-crusted concoction that has a sweet or savory filling with various toppings. Thankfully, there are many variations on the traditional flour crust, and this chapter introduces many of them. It's nice to have a gluten-free option for pie crust, and you'll find a recipe for that here too. Then there are crusts that can be made from all kinds of cookies, from graham crackers and their flavor variations, to Oreos, chocolate chip cookies, Pepperidge Farm classics like Milanos, Italian anisette cookies, and almost any other kind of cookie you can think of. I was delighted to play with nuts to create a variety of crusts, too. Nut crusts make the perfect base for pies like pumpkin, sweet potato, and even lemon or key lime.

BAKED CRUST

MAKES 1 12-INCH CRUST ✦ ACTIVE TIME: 20 MINUTES ✦ START TO FINISH: 2 HOURS

Many of the pies in this cookbook call for a simple, single baked crust. It's fast and easy to put together and the result is delicious.

1¼ cups flour

¼ teaspoon salt

½ cup (1 stick) unsalted butter, chilled and cut into small pieces, plus 1 tablespoon butter for greasing the skillet

4 to 6 tablespoons cold water

1. In a large bowl, combine the flour and salt. Add the butter and work it into the flour mixture with a pastry blender or 2 knives until the dough resembles coarse meal. Add 3 tablespoons cold water to start, and using your hands or a fork, work the dough, adding additional tablespoons until it just holds together when you gather it in your hands.

2. Working on a lightly floured surface, gather the dough and place it on the work area, forming it into a solid ball or disk. Wrap tightly in plastic wrap and refrigerate for about an hour. Dough can be refrigerated for a couple of days or frozen for a couple of months.

3. Preheat the oven to 450 degrees. Take the dough out of the refrigerator to allow it to warm up a bit but work with it cold. Put the refrigerated dough on a lightly floured surface, and with a lightly dusted rolling pin, flatten the dough into a circle, working both sides to extend it to a 12-inch round.

4. Grease the cast-iron skillet with 1 tablespoon of butter.

5. Carefully position the crust in the skillet so it is evenly distributed, pressing it in lightly. Crimp the edges. Use a fork to prick the crust on the bottom and sides.

6. Bake for 10 to 12 minutes until lightly browned. Transfer to a wire rack to cool before filling.

FLAKY PASTRY CRUST

**MAKES 2 10- TO 12- INCH CRUSTS ✦ ACTIVE TIME: 30 MINUTES ✦
START TO FINISH: 2-3 HOURS**

This is the traditional pie crust recipe, and while it's tempting to take a shortcut and use a pie crust mix or even a pre-made crust, there truly is nothing as delicious as a crust made from scratch. Once you get the hang of it, too, you'll find making the crust as enjoyable and therapeutic as indulging in the pie.

2½ cups flour

1 teaspoon salt

¼ cup vegetable shortening

½ cup (1 stick) butter, chilled and cut into small pieces (if using unsalted butter, increase salt to 1¼ teaspoons), plus 1 tablespoon butter for greasing the skillet

6 to 8 tablespoons cold water

1 tablespoon milk

1. In a large bowl, combine the flour and salt. Add the shortening, and using a fork, work it in until the mixture forms very coarse meal. Add the butter and work into the dough with a pastry blender or your fingers until the meal is just holding together. Don't overwork the dough; there can be chunks of butter in it. Add 4 tablespoons cold water to start, and using your hands or a fork, work the dough, adding additional tablespoons until it just holds together when you gather it in your hands.

2. Working on a lightly floured surface, gather the dough and place it on the work area, forming it into a solid ball. Separate into equal parts and form into disks. Wrap each tightly in plastic wrap and refrigerate for 30 to 60 minutes. Dough can be refrigerated for a couple of days or frozen for a couple of months.

3. Take the dough out of the refrigerator to allow it to warm up a bit but work with it cold. Put the refrigerated dough on a lightly floured surface, and with a lightly dusted rolling pin, flatten the dough into 2 circles, working both sides to extend each to a 10- to 12-inch round.

4. Grease the cast-iron skillet with 1 tablespoon of butter.

5. Carefully position the crust in the skillet so it is evenly distributed, pressing it in lightly and allowing the dough to extend over the side.

6. If making a single-crust pie, crimp the edges as desired. If filling and adding a top crust, leave the extra dough so it can be crimped with the top crust. Fill the pie as directed, and then roll out the top crust so it is just bigger than the diameter of the top of the skillet. For an extra flaky pastry crust, refrigerate the completed pie for about 30 minutes before baking.

7. When ready to bake, cut a slit or hole in the middle of the top crust for heat to escape. Brush the crust with milk, which will turn it a nice brown color. Bake as directed.

GLUTEN-FREE PIE CRUST

MAKES 1 12-INCH CRUST ✦ ACTIVE TIME: 20 MINUTES ✦ START TO FINISH: 90 MINUTES

Achieving something somewhat flaky is the trick with a gluten-free pie crust. This comes very close, and it's delicious, too. Double the recipe for a two-crust pie.

1¼ cups gluten-free multi-purpose flour blend

1 tablespoon sugar

½ teaspoon xanthan gum

½ teaspoon salt

6 tablespoons unsalted butter, chilled and cut into small pieces, plus 1 tablespoon butter for greasing the skillet

1 large egg

2 teaspoons fresh squeezed lemon juice

1 to 2 tablespoons cold water

1. In a large bowl, combine the flour blend, sugar, xanthan gum, and salt. Add the butter and work it into the flour mixture with a pastry blender or your fingers to form a coarse meal that includes whole bits of butter.

2. In a small bowl, whisk the egg and lemon juice together briskly until very foamy. Add to the dry ingredients and stir until the dough holds together. If dough isn't quite holding, add 1 tablespoon of cold water at a time until it does. Shape into a disk, wrap tightly in plastic wrap, and refrigerate for 30 to 60 minutes or overnight.

3. When ready to make the pie, take dough out of the refrigerator and allow to rest at room temperature for about 10 minutes before rolling. Working on a flat surface dusted with gluten-free flour, roll the dough into a 12-inch disk.

4. Grease the cast-iron skillet with 1 tablespoon of butter.

5. Carefully position the crust in the skillet so it is evenly distributed, pressing it in lightly. Crimp the edges. Fill and bake as directed.

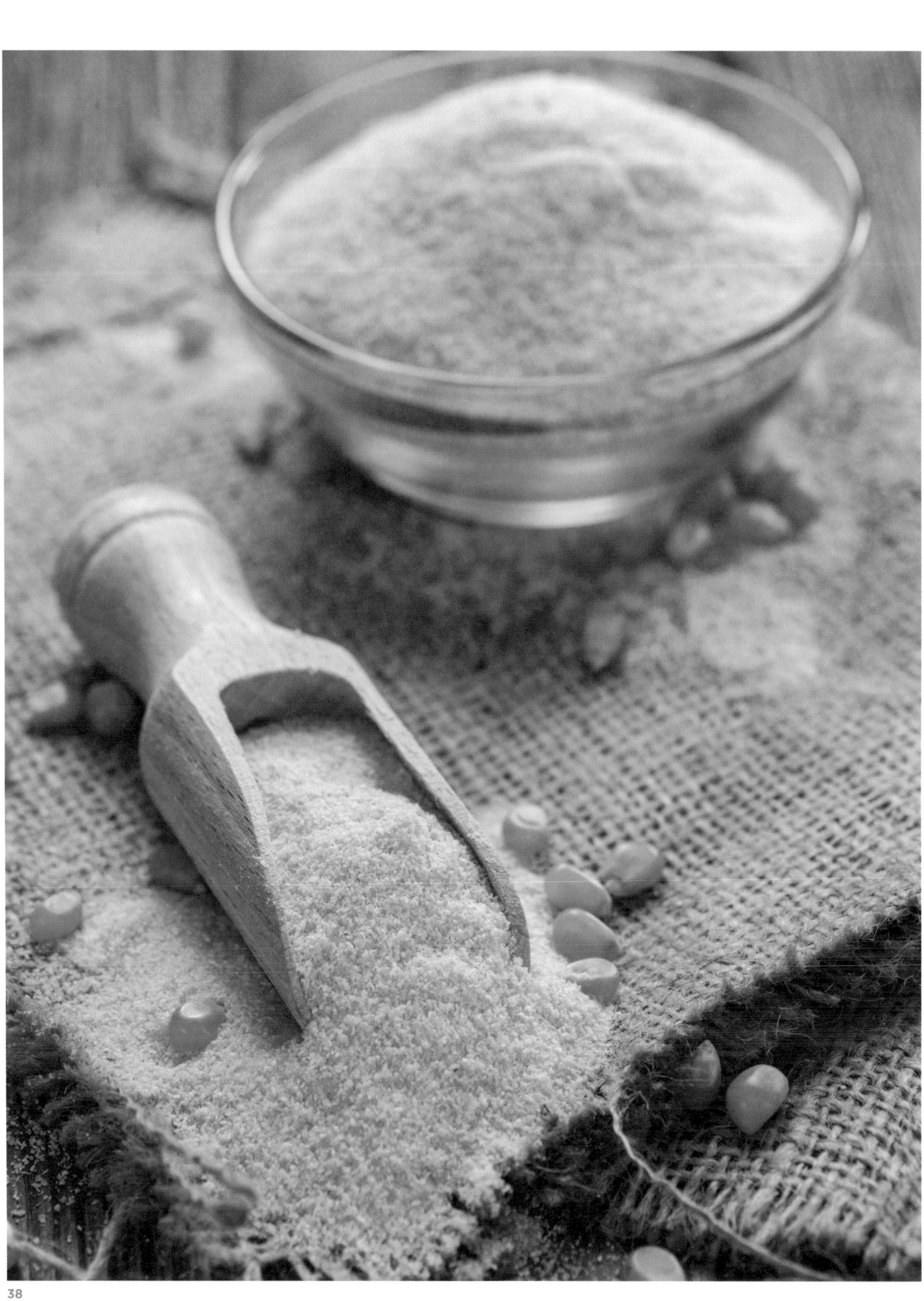

SWEET & SAVORY CORNMEAL CRUST

MAKES 1 12-INCH CRUST ✦ ACTIVE TIME: 20 MINUTES ✦ START TO FINISH: 90 MINUTES

A crust that includes cornmeal will have more texture and flavor than a crust made from simple all-purpose flour. This distinctive texture and flavor is a perfect complement to savory fillings when prepared without sugar, and makes a great base for sweet pies as well. It's easy to make, too. There are recipes for both variations in the book.

¾ cup all-purpose flour

¾ cup yellow cornmeal

3 tablespoons sugar
if making a sweet crust

½ teaspoon salt

½ cup (1 stick) unsalted
butter, chilled and cut
into small pieces, plus
1 tablespoon butter for
greasing the skillet

1 egg, slightly beaten

1. In a large bowl, thoroughly combine the flour, cornmeal, salt, and sugar if making a sweet crust. Add the butter and work it into the flour mixture with a pastry blender or your fingers to form coarse meal. Add the egg and continue to blend until the dough comes together.

2. Shape into a disk, cover tightly with plastic wrap, and refrigerate for 30 minutes.

3. Preheat the oven to 375 degrees. Take the dough out of the refrigerator to allow it to warm up a bit but work with it cold. Put the refrigerated dough on a lightly floured surface, and with a lightly dusted rolling pin, flatten the dough into a circle, working both sides to extend it to a 10- to 12-inch round.

4. Grease the cast-iron skillet with 1 tablespoon of butter.

5. Carefully position the crust in the skillet so it is evenly distributed, pressing it in lightly. Crimp the edges. Use a fork to prick the crust on the bottom and sides.

6. Bake for 10 to 12 minutes until lightly browned. Transfer to a wire rack to cool before filling.

GRAHAM CRACKER CRUST

MAKES 1 12-INCH CRUST ✦ ACTIVE TIME: 20 MINUTES ✦ START TO FINISH: 45 MINUTES

I'm a fan of crushing graham crackers to make this crust, but you can now purchase graham cracker crumbs in the baked goods aisle of your grocery store. Either works, as the cracker is held together with butter and sugar. There are so many fillings that complement the flavor and texture of a graham cracker crust. Experiment and enjoy.

1½ cups graham cracker crumbs

2 tablespoons sugar

1 tablespoon 100% natural maple syrup (preferably Grade B dark)

5 tablespoons unsalted butter, melted, plus 1 tablespoon butter for greasing the skillet

1. Preheat the oven to 375 degrees.

2. In a large bowl, combine graham cracker crumbs and sugar. Stir to combine. Add maple syrup and melted butter and stir to thoroughly combine.

3. Liberally grease the skillet with the butter. Pour the cracker crust dough into the skillet and lightly press into shape. Bake for 10 to 12 minutes until golden.

4. Allow to cool on a wire rack before filling.

Variations

❀ Chocolate Graham Cracker Crust—Use chocolate graham crackers instead of plain.

❀ Cinnamon Graham Cracker Crust—Use cinnamon graham crackers instead of plain or add ½ teaspoon ground cinnamon and ¼ teaspoon ground ginger to the basic graham cracker crust mix.

❀ Hint of Heat Graham Cracker Crust—Add ¼ to ½ teaspoon cayenne pepper to the graham crackers before adding sugar, syrup, and butter.

MERINGUE PIE SHELL

MAKES 1 12-INCH CRUST ✦ ACTIVE TIME: 30 MINUTES ✦ START TO FINISH: 90 MINUTES

Making this crust is a great way to use up egg whites left over from another recipe, or just because! The baking time is long and slow, but the result is a light, delicious, gluten-free shell that's perfect for creamy or fruit fillings.

3 egg whites at room temperature

¼ teaspoon cream of tartar

¾ cup sugar

½ teaspoon vanilla

1 tablespoon butter for greasing the skillet

1. Preheat the oven to 225 degrees.

2. In a large bowl, beat egg whites and cream of tartar on high speed until foamy. Beating constantly, add sugar 2 tablespoons at a time, beating after each addition until sugar is thoroughly dissolved before adding the next. Beat until whites are glossy and stand in stiff peaks. Add and beat in vanilla.

3. Grease the skillet with the butter and spread the meringue over it, working it up the sides to form a rim.

4. Bake for 60 to 90 minutes until meringue is firm and a toothpick inserted in center comes out clean. Turn off the oven and allow to dry and crisp in the cooling oven for at least 1 hour. Remove from oven, cool completely on a wire rack, and fill as desired.

PECAN NUT CRUST

MAKES 1 12-INCH CRUST ✦ ACTIVE TIME: 30 MINUTES ✦ START TO FINISH: 45 MINUTES

So simple and elegant and delicious, nut crusts are a great gluten-free alternative to traditional crusts. They're a great base for everything from creamy, earthy fillings like pumpkin to decadent chocolate cream and even frozen yogurt with fruit.

1½ cups raw pecans

1½ tablespoons honey

2 tablespoons unsalted butter, chilled and cut into small pieces, plus 1 tablespoon butter for greasing the skillet

1. Preheat the oven to 400 degrees.

2. Put the pecan pieces in a food processor and pulse until you have a coarse, crumbly meal. Alternately, you can put the pieces in a large, thick plastic bag and mash them with a rolling pin or meat tenderizer.

3. Transfer the crushed nuts to a bowl and add the honey and butter, mixing with a pastry blender, fork, or your fingers until a coarse meal is formed. There can be chunks of butter.

4. Liberally grease the skillet with the butter. Transfer the nut mixture to the skillet and gently press it into the pan to form a crust.

5. Put the skillet on top of a cookie sheet to catch any oil that may drip from the nuts. Bake for 10 to 12 minutes, until browned and toasty. Remove from the oven and allow to cool completely on a wire rack.

Variations

✺ Almond Crust—Substitute 1½ cups raw almonds for pecans.

✺ Walnut Crust—Substitute 1½ cups raw walnut pieces for pecans

✺ Hazelnut Crust—Use ¾ cup raw hazelnuts with ¾ cup almonds or pecans.

✺ Mixed Nut—Use a blend of all these nuts.

FRUIT PIES

Fruit pies! That's what it's all about—the quintessential, all-American PIE! Fresh fruit, sweetened, piled between two flaky pastry crusts, and often served with another all-American favorite, ice cream. It's no wonder a fruit pie captures not just the appetite but the imagination. It's a thing of beauty, with its browned edges, residues of hot fruit lava trickling through slits or lattice patterns…looking at a pie is nearly half the satisfaction of eating one.

Making a fruit pie in a cast-iron skillet takes the experience to a new level. The even heat distribution that the cast-iron skillet makes possible is great for the bottom pie crust, as crust develops lightness and flakiness from the heat working on the fat-flour combination. There's more butter needed for a pie made in a cast-iron skillet, and that's not a bad thing when flavor is involved! Last but not least, a pie served in a skillet makes for a down-to-earth presentation.

APPLE PIE

SERVES 6 TO 8 ✦ ACTIVE TIME: 60 MINUTES ✦ START TO FINISH: 2 HOURS

Impress your friends! Impress your family! Impress yourself—you won't believe how easy this is and how delicious the result!

1 flaky pastry crust recipe for a double crust (see page 35)

6 Granny Smith apples, peeled, cored, and sliced

1 teaspoon ground cinnamon

¾ cup sugar

1 teaspoon fresh squeezed lemon juice

1 tablespoon butter

1 tablespoon light brown sugar

1 egg white

1. Preheat the oven to 350 degrees.

2. In a large bowl, toss apples with cinnamon, sugar, and lemon juice.

3. Put the skillet over medium heat and melt the butter in it. Add the brown sugar and cook, stirring constantly, until sugar is dissolved, 1 or 2 minutes. Carefully remove pan from heat.

4. Place 1 of the piecrusts over the sugar mixture. Fill with the apple/spice mix, and place the other crust over the apples, crimping the edges together.

5. Brush the top crust with the egg white. Cut 4 or 5 slits in the middle.

6. Put the skillet in the oven and bake for about 60 minutes until golden brown and bubbly. Cover the outermost edge with aluminum foil in the last 10 minutes of baking to prevent it from burning.

7. Allow to cool before serving. Serve with whipped cream or ice cream.

You can flavor whipped cream with liqueur for an especially yummy topping. Beat heavy or whipping cream until soft peaks form. Add about ¼ cup sugar and continue beating until stiff peaks form. Gently beat in ¼ cup liqueur, such as apple brandy or Cointreau. Serve immediately or cover with plastic wrap and refrigerate until ready to serve.

DEEP-DISH APPLE PIE

MAKES 6 TO 8 SERVINGS ✦ ACTIVE TIME: 30 MINUTES ✦ START TO FINISH: 90 MINUTES

The key to this pie is to slice the apples thin and just layer and layer them between the flaky crusts. The result? Amazing.

1 flaky pastry crust recipe for a double crust (see page 35)

8 baking apples, such as Granny Smith, Fuji, Cortland, or Jonagold, peeled, cored, and sliced

½ teaspoon cinnamon

¼ teaspoon nutmeg

¼ teaspoon ground ginger

½ cup sugar

½ cup golden raisins

1 tablespoon fresh squeezed lemon juice

2 tablespoons flour

1 tablespoon butter, cut into bits

1. Preheat the oven to 375 degrees.

2. In a large bowl, toss apples with cinnamon, nutmeg, ginger, sugar, raisins, lemon juice, and flour, being sure to coat the pieces.

3. Transfer apple mixture to cast-iron skillet with bottom crust. Distribute evenly. Dot the top with butter. Roll out second crust to cover the pie, and lay the top crust on, crimping the edges to seal them. Lightly beat the egg yolk and use as a wash on the top crust.

4. Bake for about 60 minutes, or until bubbling.

5. Cool on a wire rack. Serve with whipped cream or ice cream.

CHERRY-APPLE PIE

MAKES 6 TO 8 SERVINGS ✦ ACTIVE TIME: 45 MINUTES ✦ START TO FINISH: 90 MINUTES

Cherries add a bit of tang and a refreshing texture to a more traditional apple pie. This one uses canned cherry pie filling and is really easy to make.

1 baked crust (see page 32)

3 large apples, peeled, cored, and sliced

1 tablespoon butter

1 tablespoon fresh squeezed lemon juice

¼ teaspoon ground ginger

1 (15-oz.) can cherry pie filling

1. Preheat the oven to 350 degrees.

2. In a skillet or sauté pan over medium heat, combine apple pieces with butter and cook, stirring, until apple pieces soften, about 10 minutes.

3. Transfer apple pieces to a large bowl and add lemon juice, ground ginger, and cherry pie filling. Stir to combine well.

4. Put apple/cherry filling into crust.

5. Bake for 20 to 25 minutes until heated through and set. Allow to cool slightly and serve with vanilla ice cream.

APPLE-PEAR PIE

MAKES 6 TO 8 SERVINGS ✦ ACTIVE TIME: 30 MINUTES ✦ START TO FINISH: 90 MINUTES

Using a combination of apples and pears results in a pie that's not quite as sweet as an apples-only pie. Dark brown sugar instead of light brown sugar also contributes to the earthiness.

1 flaky pastry crust recipe for a double crust (see page 35)

3 Granny Smith apples, peeled, cored, and sliced

3 firm pears (Anjou or Bartlett), peeled, cored, and sliced

½ teaspoon ground cinnamon

½ teaspoon ground nutmeg

½ cup sugar

1 teaspoon fresh squeezed lemon juice

1 tablespoon flour

1 tablespoon butter

1 tablespoon dark brown sugar

1 egg white

1. Preheat the oven to 350 degrees.

2. In a large bowl, toss fruit with cinnamon, nutmeg, sugar, lemon juice, and flour, being sure to coat the pieces.

3. Put the skillet over medium heat and melt the butter in it. Add the brown sugar and cook, stirring constantly, until sugar is dissolved, 1 or 2 minutes. Carefully remove pan from heat.

4. Place 1 of the piecrusts over the sugar mixture. Fill with the apple-pear mix, and place the other crust over the fruit, crimping the edges together.

5. Brush the top crust with the egg white. Cut 4 or 5 slits in the middle.

6. Put the skillet in the oven and bake for 60 to 70 minutes until golden brown and bubbly. Cover the outermost edge with aluminum foil in the last 10 minutes of baking to prevent it from burning.

7. Allow to cool before serving. Serve with whipped cream or ice cream.

NUTTY APPLE-CRANBERRY PIE

SERVES 6 TO 8 ◆ **ACTIVE TIME: 60 MINUTES** ◆ **START TO FINISH: 2 HOURS**

If you and your family like something a bit sweet-tart, you'll love this pie. The sweetness of the apples pairs wonderfully with the tartness of fresh cranberries, and the toasted walnuts add a buttery earthiness

1 flaky pastry crust recipe for a double crust (see page 35)

1 cup chopped walnuts

6 Granny Smith apples, peeled, cored, and sliced

1 cup fresh cranberries

1 teaspoon ground cinnamon

¼ teaspoon nutmeg

¼ teaspoon ground ginger

1 cup sugar

1 teaspoon fresh squeezed lemon juice

2 tablespoons butter

2 tablespoons light brown sugar

1 egg white

1 tablespoon sugar

1. Preheat the oven to 450 degrees.

2. Spread the walnut pieces out on a cookie sheet and bake until toasted, about 5 to 8 minutes, removing the cookie sheet mid-way to shake and turn the nuts. Keep an eye on them so they don't burn. Remove the cookie sheet from the oven and allow the nuts to cool. Reduce the oven temperature to 350 degrees.

3. In a large bowl, toss apples with cranberries, cinnamon, nutmeg, ginger, sugar, and lemon juice. Stir in the walnut pieces.

4. Put the skillet over medium heat and melt the butter in it. Add the brown sugar and cook, stirring constantly, until sugar is dissolved, 1 or 2 minutes. Carefully remove pan from heat.

5. Place 1 of the piecrusts over the sugar mixture. Fill with the apple/cranberry mix, and place the other crust over the apples, crimping the edges together.

6. Brush the top crust with the egg white, and sprinkle the sugar over it. Cut 4 or 5 slits in the middle.

7. Put the skillet in the oven and bake for 60 to 70 minutes until golden brown and bubbly. Cover the outermost edge with aluminum foil in the last 10 minutes of baking to prevent it from burning.

8. Allow to cool before serving.

APPLE-CRANBERRY PIE WITH POMEGRANATE SAUCE

MAKES 6 TO 8 SERVINGS ✦ ACTIVE TIME: 60 MINUTES ✦ START TO FINISH: 2 HOURS

This is the perfect pie for Thanksgiving, as it combines the fruits synonymous with late fall and the celebration of the harvest. The pomegranate sauce is the key to bringing it all together.

1 flaky pastry crust recipe for a single crust (see page 35)

6 to 8 crisp-tart apples such as Macoun, Granny Smith, or Jonah Gold, peeled, cored, and cut into small pieces

3 tablespoons butter

2 tablespoons flour

½ cup light brown sugar

1 teaspoon cinnamon

¼ teaspoon nutmeg

¼ teaspoon salt

1 cup whole cranberries

1 tablespoon butter

Sauce

½ cup pomegranate juice (unsweetened)

1 cup frozen pomegranate seeds

¼ cup sugar

1 tablespoon fresh squeezed lemon juice

1. Preheat the oven to 375 degrees.

2. In a large pot, melt the butter. When melted, add the apples, flour, sugar, cinnamon, nutmeg, and salt. Stir to combine. Cook, stirring over medium heat until apples just start to soften, about 3 minutes. Stir in the cranberries and continue to cook, stirring, for another 2 minutes.

3. Put the skillet over medium heat and melt the butter in it. Carefully remove pan from heat.

4. Place the piecrust in the skillet. Fill with the apple/cranberry mix. Bake for 20 minutes.

5. While the pie is baking, make the pomegranate sauce. In a saucepan over medium-high heat, cook the pomegranate juice until it's reduced slightly, stirring occasionally, about 5 minutes. Stir in the pomegranate seeds, sugar, and lemon juice. Continue to cook, stirring, until seeds are thawed, another 5 minutes or so.

6. Remove pie from oven and pour sauce over the top. Return to the oven and finish baking, another 15 minutes or so, until bubbling.

7. Allow to cool before serving. Serve with vanilla ice cream!

APPLE-RASPBERRY PIE

MAKES 6 TO 8 SERVINGS ✦ ACTIVE TIME: 35 MINUTES ✦ START TO FINISH: 90 MINUTES

The sweet summery taste of fresh raspberries makes for a lovely pairing with apples. If you're inspired, make a lattice crust on this one so the dark liquid of the cooked raspberries bubbles up in the gaps. This makes for a divine presentation.

1 flaky pastry crust recipe for a double crust (see page 35)

6 to 8 crisp-tart apples such as Macoun, Granny Smith, or Jonah Gold, peeled, cored, and sliced

2 tablespoons flour

¼ cup light brown sugar

¼ teaspoon salt

¼ cup unsweetened raspberry preserves

1 cup fresh raspberries

1 tablespoon butter

1 egg white

2 tablespoons sugar

1. Preheat the oven to 350 degrees.

2. In a large bowl, toss apples with the flour, brown sugar, and salt, being sure to coat the pieces. Add the raspberry preserves and stir. Add the fresh raspberries last, gently stirring so as not to overly macerate the fresh fruit.

3. Put the skillet over medium heat and melt the butter in it. Carefully remove pan from heat.

4. Place 1 of the piecrusts in the skillet. Fill with fruit mix.

5. Roll out the top crust on a lightly floured surface, and cut 8 strips from the dough. Arrange them in an over-under lattice pattern, crimping the edges to connect them to the bottom crust.

6. Brush the top crust with the egg white, and sprinkle the sugar over it. Cut 4 or 5 slits in the middle.

7. Cover with foil and bake for about 35 minutes. Remove the foil and finish baking, another 25 to 30 minutes, until golden and bubbling.

8. Allow to cool before serving.

MAPLE APPLE PIE

MAKES 6 TO 8 SERVINGS ✦ ACTIVE TIME: 30 MINUTES ✦ START TO FINISH: 90 MINUTES

Maple syrup is the perfect complement to apples, and is a great replacement for sugar.

1 flaky pastry crust recipe for a double crust (see page 35)

6 Granny Smith apples, peeled, cored, and sliced

1 teaspoon ground cinnamon

¼ cup 100% natural maple syrup (preferably Grade B dark)

1 teaspoon fresh squeezed lemon juice

1 tablespoon butter

1 egg white

2 tablespoons sugar

1. Preheat the oven to 350 degrees.

2. In a large bowl, toss apples with cinnamon, maple syrup, and lemon juice.

3. Put the skillet over medium heat and melt the butter in it. Carefully remove pan from heat.

4. Place 1 of the piecrusts in the skillet. Fill with the apples, and place the other crust over the apples, crimping the edges together.

5. Brush the top crust with the egg white, and sprinkle the sugar over it. Cut 4 or 5 slits in the middle.

6. Put the skillet in the oven and bake for about 60 minutes until golden brown and bubbly. Cover the outermost edge with aluminum foil in the last 10 minutes of baking to prevent it from burning.

7. Allow to cool before serving. Serve with whipped cream or ice cream.

APPLE-PEACH-BLUEBERRY PIE

SERVES 6 TO 8 ✦ ACTIVE TIME: 60 MINUTES ✦ START TO FINISH: 2 HOURS

When I was looking for ways to load up a pie with some of my very favorite fruits, I came across a variation of this recipe. I played around with it a little, and it's now one I use often when apples are in season. It's easy and yummy.

1 flaky pastry crust recipe for a double crust (see page 35)

4 cups peeled, cored, and sliced crisp-tart apples, such as Jonagold, Granny Smith, or Macoun

2 cups peeled, pitted, and sliced fresh peaches or 1 (29-oz.) can sliced peaches, drained

1 tablespoon fresh squeezed lemon juice

¾ cup granulated sugar

1 tablespoon cornstarch

½ teaspoon salt

½ teaspoon cinnamon

½ cup fresh blueberries

½ teaspoon vanilla

1 tablespoon butter, plus ¼ cup (4 tablespoons) unsalted butter for dotting top of pie filling

¼ cup 100% natural maple syrup (preferably Grade B dark)

1 teaspoon half-and-half

1. Preheat the oven to 400 degrees.

2. In a large bowl, stir together the apples and peaches with the lemon juice. In another bowl, stir together the sugar, cornstarch, salt, and cinnamon. Add to the bowl with the apples and peaches and toss to mix well. Stir in the blueberries and the vanilla.

3. Put the skillet over medium heat and melt the butter in it. Carefully remove pan from heat.

4. Place 1 of the piecrusts in the skillet. Fill with fruit mix. Cut the butter into slivers and dot the top of the fruit mix with the butter. Drizzle the maple syrup over the top. Place the other crust over the fruit, crimping the edges together.

5. Brush the top crust with the half-and-half. Cut 5 or 6 slits in the middle.

6. Cover the pie with foil and bake for 30 minutes. Remove the foil, reduce the oven temperature to 350 degrees, and bake another 35 to 40 minutes until the top is golden brown.

7. Allow to cool before serving. Serve with peach ice cream and caramel sauce for a real treat!

CHEDDAR APPLE PIE

MAKES 6 TO 8 SERVINGS ✦ ACTIVE TIME: 45 MINUTES ✦ START TO FINISH: 2 HOURS

Cheddar cheese adds a savory "something" to an apple pie. You can add the grated cheese to the crust when you make it, or you can add it directly to the apples and spices. I prefer to do this, as I like the bits of cheese in the pie itself.

1 flaky pastry crust recipe for a double crust (see page 35)

6 crisp-tart apples such as Macoun, peeled, cored, and sliced

¾ cup light brown sugar

2 tablespoons flour

¼ teaspoon salt

1 cup sharp cheddar cheese, shredded or cut into small pieces

1 tablespoon butter

1 egg white

2 tablespoons sugar

1. Preheat the oven to 350 degrees.

2. In a large bowl, toss apples with light brown sugar, flour, and salt, being sure to coat the pieces. Add and stir in the cheese.

3. Put the skillet over medium heat and melt the butter in it. Carefully remove pan from heat.

4. Place 1 of the piecrusts in the skillet. Fill with the apples, and place the other crust over the apples, crimping the edges together.

5. Brush the top crust with the egg white, and sprinkle the sugar over it. Cut 4 or 5 slits in the middle.

6. Put the skillet in the oven and bake for about 60 minutes until golden brown and bubbly. Cover the outermost edge with aluminum foil in the last 10 minutes of baking to prevent it from burning.

7. Allow to cool before serving. Serve with whipped cream or ice cream.

PEACH PIE

SERVES 6 TO 8 ✦ ACTIVE TIME: 60 MINUTES ✦ START TO FINISH: 2 HOURS

There's something otherworldly about a pie made with fresh peaches. It is just so good! With the way the cast-iron skillet yields a sugary, somewhat crunchy bottom crust, this will become your go-to recipe when peaches are in season.

1 flaky pastry crust recipe for a double crust (see page 35)

2-3 pounds peaches to yield 4 cups, peeled (see step 2), cored, and sliced

1 teaspoon fresh squeezed lemon juice

¾ cup sugar

4 tablespoons flour

1 tablespoon butter

2 tablespoons light brown sugar

1 egg white

2 tablespoons sugar

1. Preheat the oven to 350 degrees.

2. Bring a large pot of water to boil. Fill another large pot with cold water. When the water's boiling, submerge the peaches for a minute or two, then remove them with a slotted spoon and put them immediately into the cold water. This loosens the skin and makes them much easier to peel. Use enough peaches to yield 4 cups of peeled slices. In a large bowl, toss peaches with lemon juice, sugar, and flour, being sure to coat the pieces.

3. Put the skillet over medium heat and melt the butter in it. Add the brown sugar and cook, stirring constantly, until sugar is dissolved, 1 or 2 minutes. Carefully remove pan from heat.

4. Place 1 of the piecrusts over the sugar mixture. Fill with the peaches, and place the other crust over the peaches, crimping the edges together.

5. Brush the top crust with the egg white, and sprinkle the sugar over it. Cut 4 or 5 slits in the middle.

6. Put the skillet in the oven and bake for 60 to 70 minutes until golden brown and bubbly. Cover the outermost edge with aluminum foil in the last 10 minutes of baking to prevent it from burning.

7. Allow to cool before serving. Serve with bourbon whipped cream.

For this pie you have to try serving it with bourbon whipped cream. You'll understand why this is so popular in the south, from whence the best peaches—and bourbon—hail. Simply beat heavy or whipping cream until soft peaks form. Add about ¼ cup sugar and continue beating until stiff peaks form. Gently beat in ¼ cup bourbon. Serve immediately or cover with plastic wrap and refrigerate until ready to serve.

BLUEBERRY PIE

SERVES 6 TO 8 ✦ ACTIVE TIME: 30 MINUTES ✦ START TO FINISH: 90 MINUTES

Blueberry pie is so easy to make and tastes so good with rich, creamy vanilla ice cream. Summer in a slice!

1 flaky pastry crust recipe for a double crust (see page 35)

4 cups fresh or frozen blueberries

1 tablespoon fresh squeezed lemon juice

1 cup sugar

3 tablespoons flour

1 tablespoon butter

2 tablespoons brown sugar

1 egg white

2 tablespoons sugar

1. Preheat the oven to 350 degrees.

2. If using frozen blueberries, it's not necessary to thaw them completely. In a large bowl, toss blueberries with lemon juice, sugar, and flour, being sure to coat the pieces.

3. Put the skillet over medium heat and melt the butter in it. Add the brown sugar and cook, stirring constantly, until sugar is dissolved, 1 or 2 minutes. Carefully remove pan from heat.

4. Place 1 of the piecrusts over the sugar mixture. Fill with blueberries, and place the other crust over the blueberries, crimping the edges together.

5. Brush the top crust with the egg white, and sprinkle the sugar over it. Cut 4 or 5 slits in the middle.

6. Put the skillet in the oven and bake for 45 minutes until golden brown and bubbly. Cover the outermost edge with aluminum foil in the last 10 minutes of baking to prevent it from burning.

7. Allow to cool before serving.

BLUEBERRY-GINGER PIE

SERVES 6 TO 8 ✦ ACTIVE TIME: 45 MINUTES ✦ START TO FINISH: 90 MINUTES

I'm a big fan of ginger. I love its spiciness and freshness. It adds zing, and it's also really good for you. Ginger has been used for digestive upset for centuries, and also has known anti-inflammatory compounds that can help relieve joint pain. Not that a piece of this pie will cure your ills, but it's not the worst thing you could eat!

1 flaky pastry crust recipe for a double crust (see page 35)

5 cups fresh blueberries

½ cup sugar

1 tablespoon finely chopped or grated fresh ginger

2 tablespoons quick-cooking tapioca

1 teaspoon grated lemon peel

1 tablespoon fresh squeezed lemon juice

1 tablespoon butter

1 teaspoon half-and-half

¼ cup sugar

1. Preheat the oven to 400 degrees.

2. In a large bowl, toss blueberries with the sugar, ginger, tapioca, lemon peel, and lemon juice.

3. Put the skillet over medium heat and melt the butter in it. Carefully remove pan from heat.

4. Place 1 of the piecrusts in the skillet. Fill with blueberry mix, and place the other crust over the fruit, crimping the edges together.

5. Brush the top crust with the half-and-half, and sprinkle the sugar over it. Cut 4 or 5 slits in the middle.

6. Place foil or cookie sheet on oven rack below middle rack to catch any spills. Put the skillet in the oven and bake for 35 to 40 minutes until golden brown and bubbly. Cover the outermost edge with aluminum foil in the last 10 minutes of baking to prevent it from burning.

7. Cool at least 2 hours before serving. Serve warm or cold.

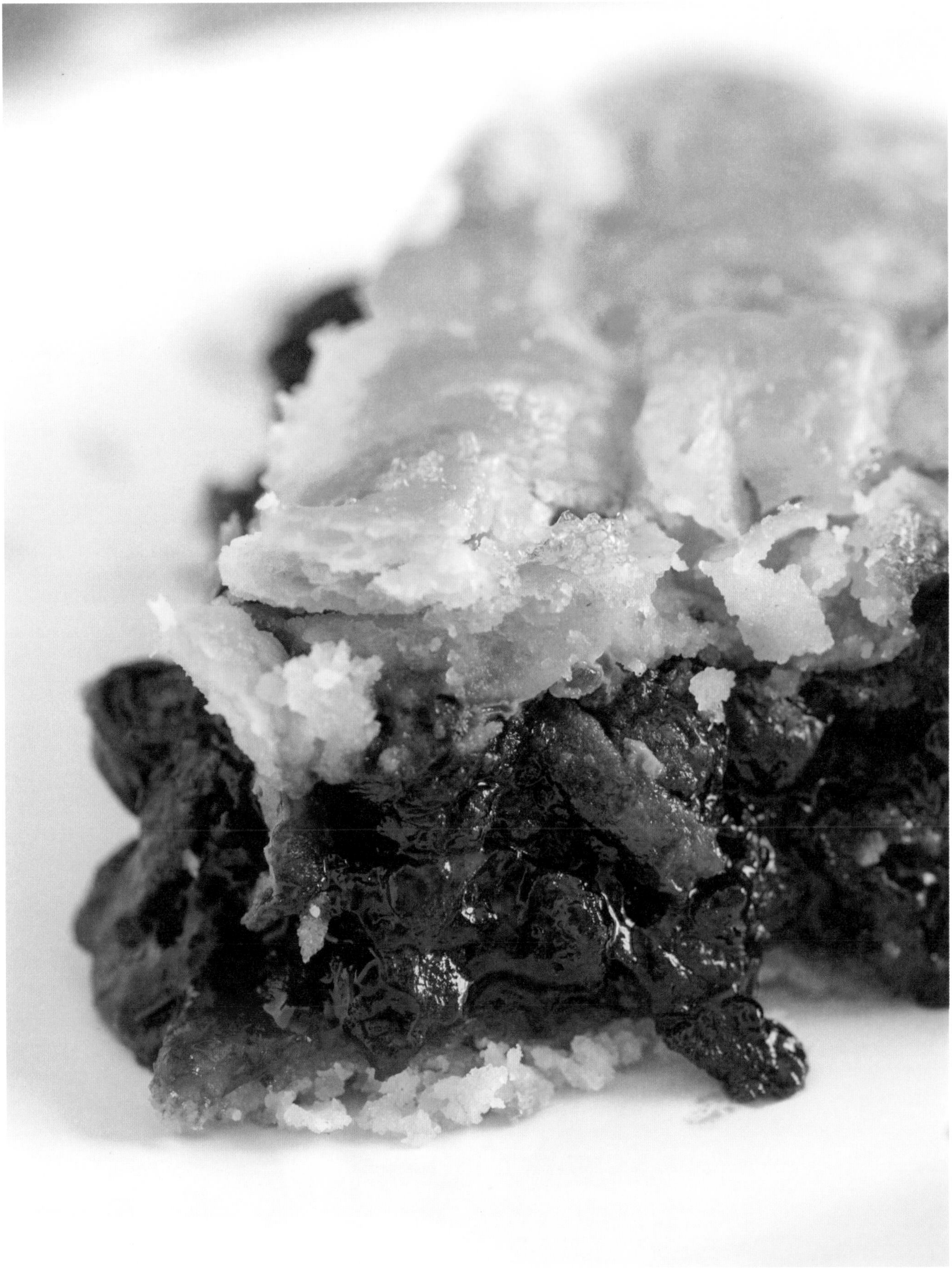

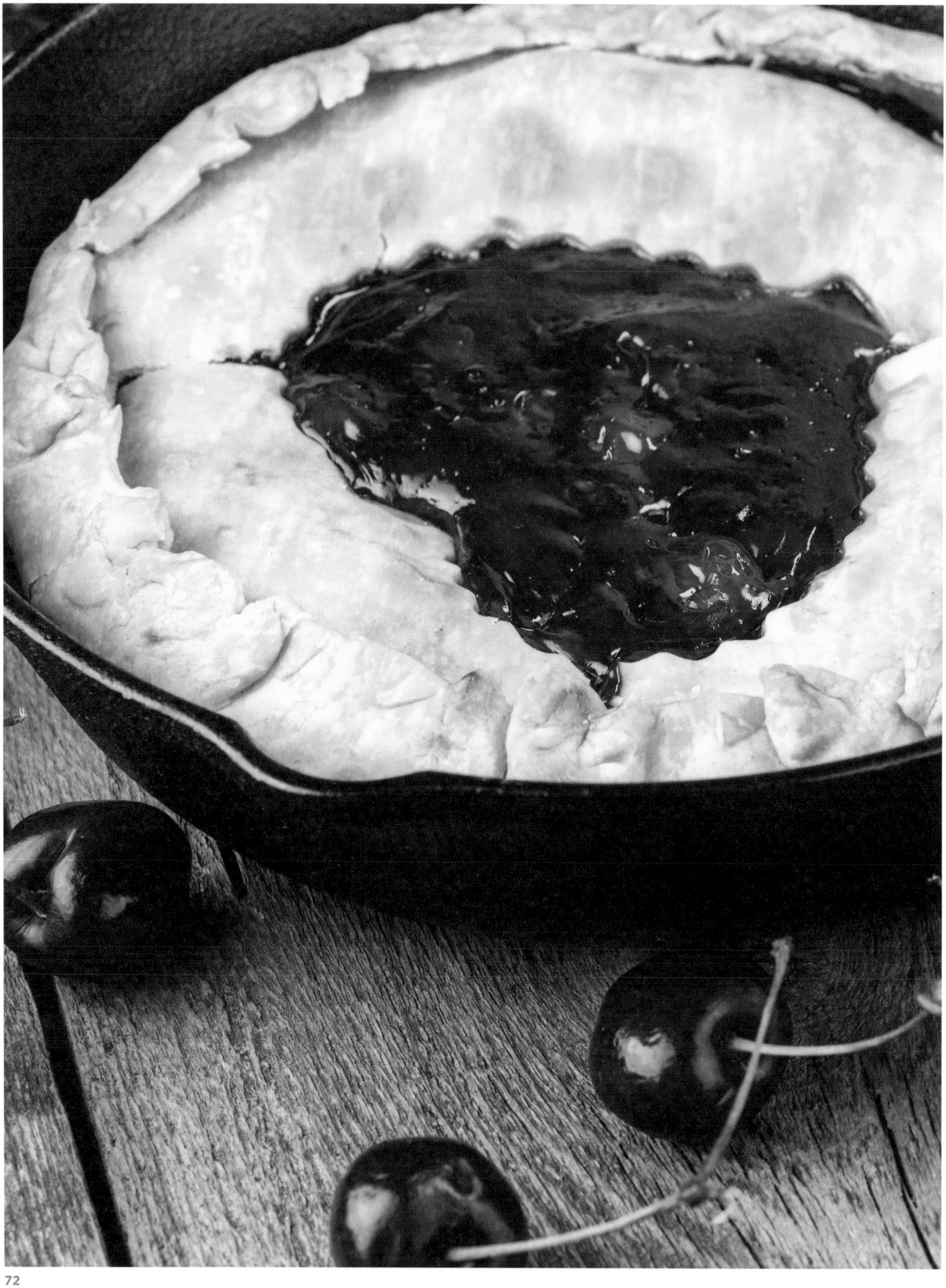

VERY CHERRY PIE

What I love about making this pie is working with the cherries. It takes time to slice and pit them, and I use this time to whet my appetite for the final result by eating cherries as I work. A few for the pie, a few for me…the simple things! I also prefer to only use fresh cherries for pie, as there is no substitute for the flavor. Use one variety or a combination.

1 flaky pastry crust recipe for a single crust (see page 35)

4 cups fresh cherries, pitted (see step 2)

1 tablespoon fresh squeezed lemon juice

1 cup sugar

1½ tablespoons flour

2 tablespoons butter

2 tablespoons brown sugar

1 egg white

2 tablespoons sugar

1. Preheat the oven to 350 degrees.

2. Pitting the cherries takes time, but it's worth it. Work with clean cherries and put a piece of waxed paper over the area where you'll be working, as the juice will drip and stain. Have your measuring cup ready to put the cherries in when they're pitted. Use toothpicks or tweezers with a pointed end or the kind of tool to get lobster meat out of the shell—something small and sharp on the end. Remove the stem from the cherry, insert the toothpick or tool next to the pit, and circle the pit until it can be scooped out.

3. When you have 4 cups of pitted cherries, put them in a large bowl and toss with lemon juice, sugar and flour, being sure to coat the pieces.

4. Put the skillet over medium heat and melt the butter in it. Add the brown sugar and cook, stirring constantly, until sugar is dissolved, 1 or 2 minutes. Carefully remove pan from heat.

5. Place 1 of the piecrusts over the sugar mixture. Fill with the cherries.

6. Put the skillet in the oven and bake for 50 to 60 minutes until golden brown and bubbly. Cover the outermost edge with aluminum foil in the last 10 minutes of baking to prevent it from burning.

7. Allow to cool before serving.

CHERRY PEARY PIE

SERVES 6 TO 8 ✦ ACTIVE TIME: 60 MINUTES ✦ START TO FINISH: 90 MINUTES

It's fun just to say the name of this pie. What's even nicer is the tart cherry alongside the mellow pear. The graham cracker crust adds crunch and texture. A winner!

1 graham cracker crust (see page 40)

3 ripe pears, peeled, cored, and cut into bite-sized pieces

1 teaspoon fresh squeezed lemon juice

¾ cup sugar

2 tablespoons cornstarch

1 cup fresh sour cherries, pitted and halved (if fresh cherries aren't available, search for canned sour cherries)

2 tablespoons unsalted butter, cut into slivers

1. Preheat the oven to 350 degrees.

2. In a large bowl, combine pear pieces with lemon juice, sugar, and cornstarch. Put half the fruit into the graham cracker crust.

3. Arrange the sour cherries on top of the pear mixture, and top with the remaining pear mixture. Dot the pie with the butter slivers.

4. Cover the pie with foil and bake for 20 minutes. Remove the foil and continue to bake for another 15 to 20 minutes until the topping is golden brown and bubbly.

5. Allow to cool before serving, and serve with vanilla ice cream.

BLACKBERRY-PEACH PIE

SERVES 6 TO 8 ✦ ACTIVE TIME: 60 MINUTES ✦ START TO FINISH: 2 HOURS

Colorful and flavorful, and smacking of summer, this is the perfect pie for nights when the sun doesn't set until after 9. Ah, summertime!

1 flaky pastry crust recipe for a double crust (see page 35)

4 cups fresh peaches, peeled, pitted, and cut into pieces (see page 66)

¾ cup sugar

3 tablespoons flour

½ teaspoon grated lemon peel

1 tablespoon fresh squeezed lemon juice

¼ teaspoon ground ginger

1 cup fresh blackberries

1 tablespoon butter

1 egg white

2 tablespoons sugar

1. Preheat the oven to 375 degrees.

2. In a large bowl, toss peaches with sugar, flour, lemon peel, lemon juice, and ginger. Gently stir in blackberries.

3. Put the skillet over medium heat and melt the butter in it. Carefully remove pan from heat.

4. Place 1 of the piecrusts in the skillet. Fill with fruit mix. Roll out the top crust on a lightly floured surface, and cut 8 strips from the dough. Arrange them in an over-under lattice pattern, crimping the edges to connect them to the bottom crust, or use whole and cut 4-5 slits in the top.

5. Brush the top crust with the egg white, and sprinkle the sugar over it.

6. Put the skillet in the oven and bake for about 55 to 60 minutes, until golden brown and bubbly

7. Allow to cool before serving, and top with fresh whipped cream.

GRAPE PIE

SERVES 6 TO 8 ✦ ACTIVE TIME: 60 MINUTES ✦ START TO FINISH: 90 MINUTES

A refreshing twist on tarte tatin, though it's a similar concept: fruit embedded in pastry cream. Sliced grapes make a beautiful presentation, and the taste is just as nice. Serve with a white dessert wine, like an Ice Wine.

1 flaky pastry crust recipe for a single crust (see page 35)

1 (10-oz.) jar lemon curd

1 tablespoon fresh squeezed lemon juice

1 teaspoon lemon zest

1 tablespoon butter

1 tablespoon light brown sugar

2-3 cups seedless grapes, sliced in half (white, red or a combination)

2 tablespoons sugar

1. Preheat the oven to 350 degrees.

2. In a small bowl, combine the lemon curd, lemon juice, and lemon zest. Set aside.

3. Put the skillet over medium heat and melt the butter in it. Add the brown sugar and cook, stirring constantly, until sugar is dissolved, 1 or 2 minutes. Carefully remove pan from heat.

4. Place the piecrust over the sugar mixture. Spread the lemon curd mix over the piecrust. Place the grape halves in a decorative pattern on top of the lemon curd, skin side up. Sprinkle with sugar.

5. Put the skillet in the oven and bake for 45 to 50 minutes until set.

6. Allow to cool before serving.

STRAWBERRY PIE

SERVES 6 TO 8 ✦ ACTIVE TIME: 40 MINUTES ✦ START TO FINISH: 4 HOURS

If you just can't get enough strawberries in early summer, this pie will surely satisfy. Topped with strawberry preserves, it's absolutely heavenly.

1 baked crust (see page 32)

6 cups (about 3 pints) fresh strawberries, washed, tops trimmed, and sliced in half or quarters

¾ cup sugar

3 tablespoons cornstarch

½ cup water

½ cup unsweetened strawberry preserves

1. In a saucepan over medium heat, mix sugar, cornstarch, and water. Stir in 1 cup of strawberry pieces. Cook, stirring until mixture begins to boil and thicken. Continue to cook and stir for about 5 minutes. Remove from the heat and allow to cool, about 20 minutes

2. Spread the remaining strawberry pieces evenly in the pie crust. When cooked mixture is cool, pour it over the larger pieces of fruit.

3. In a microwave-proof bowl, melt the strawberry preserves until just melted, about 20 seconds. Stir and drizzle the melted jam over the pie to distribute evenly.

4. Cover with plastic wrap and refrigerate for at least 3 hours and up to 1 day. Serve with whipped cream or ice cream (strawberry, vanilla, or another fruit flavor).

STRAWBERRY-RHUBARB PIE

SERVES 6 TO 8 ✦ ACTIVE TIME: 45 MINUTES ✦ START TO FINISH: 2 HOURS

In the spring, Rhubarb is one of the earliest things to reappear in the gardens of those of us who live in the Northeast, and so it is celebrated. Rhubarb is naturally tart, which is why it works so well with strawberries, which, when fresh, are bursting with sweetness.

1 flaky pastry crust recipe for a double crust (see page 35)

4-5 stalks rhubarb, cleaned and cut into 1-inch pieces (use about 1½ pounds frozen rhubarb, thawed, if fresh isn't available)

1 quart fresh strawberries, washed and tops trimmed, and sliced in half or quarters (use ½ pound frozen strawberries, thawed, if fresh aren't available)

¾ cup sugar

⅓ cup flour

1 tablespoon butter

1 egg white

1. Preheat the oven to 375 degrees.

2. In a large bowl, toss rhubarb and strawberries with sugar and flour.

3. Put the skillet over medium heat and melt the butter in it. Carefully remove pan from heat.

4. Place 1 of the piecrusts in the skillet. Fill with rhubarb/strawberry mix, and place the other crust over the fruit, crimping the edges together.

5. Brush the top crust with the egg white. Cut 4 or 5 slits in the middle.

6. Put the skillet in the oven and bake for about 45 to 55 minutes until golden brown and bubbly. Cover the outermost edge with aluminum foil in the last 10 minutes of baking to prevent it from burning.

7. Allow to cool before serving. Serve with whipped cream.

MIXED BERRY PIE

SERVES 6 TO 8 ✦ ACTIVE TIME: 30 MINUTES ✦ START TO FINISH: 90 MINUTES

I especially like this pie in a cornmeal crust. It gives it extra texture since the berries soften as they cook. Try it with this or a regular crust and see which you prefer. Of course, it's best to use all fresh fruit, but if one of them isn't available, you can substitute frozen fruit (thaw it first).

1 cornmeal crust
(see page 39)

1½ cups fresh
blueberries

1 cup fresh blackberries

1 cup fresh raspberries

1½ cups fresh
strawberries, washed
and tops trimmed, and
sliced in half

1 tablespoon fresh
lemon juice

½ cup light brown sugar

2 tablespoons
cornstarch

½ cup unsweetened
raspberry preserves

1. Preheat oven to 375 degrees.

2. In a large bowl, toss berries with lemon juice, brown sugar, and cornstarch. Transfer fruit to a large saucepan and cook over medium heat for about 3 minutes, until the fruit just starts to warm and break down.

3. Scrape fruit and resulting juices into pie crust.

4. In a small bowl, stir the preserves until slightly liquefied. Drizzle over pie.

5. Put the skillet in the oven and bake for about 30 to 40 minutes until bubbling.

6. Allow to cool before serving. Serve with fresh whipped cream.

NECTARINE-PLUM PIE

SERVES 6 TO 8 ✦ ACTIVE TIME: 45 MINUTES ✦ START TO FINISH: 90 MINUTES

There's something sublime about this pie. I think it's the addition of Amaretto, which imparts a sweet nuttiness that's the perfect complement to the fruits.

1 flaky pastry crust recipe for a double crust (see page 35)

6 to 8 medium nectarines, peeled, pitted, and sliced into ¼-inch slices

6 to 8 fresh plums, pitted and quartered

¾ cup light brown sugar

¼ cup flour

3 tablespoons Amaretto liqueur

1 tablespoon butter, plus 3 tablespoons cold, unsalted butter for dotting top of pie filling

1 tablespoon half-and-half

1. Preheat the oven to 400 degrees.

2. In a large bowl, combine the nectarine and plum pieces. Toss with the brown sugar, flour, and Amaretto.

3. Put the skillet over medium heat and melt the butter in it. Carefully remove pan from heat.

4. Place 1 of the piecrusts in the skillet. Fill with fruit mix. Cut the butter into slivers and dot the top of the fruit mix with the butter. Place the other crust over the fruit, crimping the edges together.

5. Brush the top crust with the half-and-half.

6. Put the skillet in the oven and bake for about 40 minutes, until golden brown and bubbly.

7. Allow to cool before serving.

GLUTEN-FREE PLUM PIE

SERVES 6 TO 8 ✦ ACTIVE TIME: 45 MINUTES ✦ START TO FINISH: 3 HOURS

There's something so simple and fresh about this pie, that putting it into a gluten-free crust feels that much healthier. Of course, if you don't need or want to, you can use a regular crust. Whichever you choose, you'll discover that this is really good!

1 gluten-free crust recipe (see page 36)

10 to 12 fresh plums, washed, pitted, and quartered

½ cup granulated sugar

2 tablespoons gluten-free flour

¼ teaspoon ground nutmeg

1 tablespoon fresh squeezed lemon juice

2 tablespoons cold unsalted butter, cut into slivers

2 tablespoons half-and-half

2 tablespoons sugar

Confectioners' sugar for dusting (optional)

1. When the bottom crust is prepared in the skillet, put it in the refrigerator for 30 minutes.

2. In a large bowl, toss the plums with the sugar, gluten-free flour, nutmeg, and lemon juice. Put them in the cold bottom crust and dot with butter slivers.

3. Brush with the half-and-half, and sprinkle with sugar. Refrigerate for another 30 minutes or longer.

4. While it's refrigerating, preheat the oven to 375 degrees.

5. Put the skillet in the oven and bake for about 40 minutes, until golden, bubbly, and the plums are tender.

6. Allow to cool before serving. Dust with confectioners' sugar if desired.

SOUR CREAM PEAR-WALNUT PIE

SERVES 6 TO 8 ✦ ACTIVE TIME: 60 MINUTES ✦ START TO FINISH: 2 HOURS

Creamy, fruity, nutty....this pie is a potpourri of deliciousness. Be sure the pears you use are ripe, or substitute canned pears.

1 flaky pastry crust recipe for a single crust (see page 35)

1¼ cups sour cream

¾ cup granulated sugar

¼ cup flour

¼ teaspoon salt

2 teaspoons vanilla

1 egg

4 to 5 cups peeled, cored, and sliced ripe pears or 2 (15-oz.) cans pear slices in natural or unsweetened syrup, drained

½ cup flour

½ cup chopped walnuts

3 tablespoons 100% natural maple syrup (preferably Grade B dark)

¼ cup packed light brown sugar

½ teaspoon ground cardamom

⅛ teaspoon salt

3 tablespoons cold butter, cut into slivers

1. Preheat the oven to 400 degrees.

2. In a large bowl, whisk together the sour cream, sugar, flour, salt, vanilla, and egg until combined. Stir in the pear slices. Transfer the fruit mixture to the crust in the skillet.

3. In a separate bowl, mix the flour, walnuts, maple syrup, brown sugar, cardamom, and salt. Add butter slivers and work into nut/sugar mix with a fork or pastry blender to form coarse crumbs. Keep in refrigerator until ready to use.

4. Put the skillet in the oven and bake for 15 minutes, then reduce the oven temperature to 350 degrees and bake for another 30 minutes.

5. Remove pie from oven, take topping out of the refrigerator, and sprinkle it over the pie. Bake another 20 to 25 minutes until topping is golden brown.

6. Allow to cool before serving.

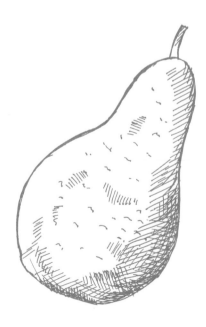

PUMPKIN PIE

SERVES 6 TO 8 ✦ ACTIVE TIME: 30 MINUTES ✦ START TO FINISH: 90 MINUTES

With the butter/sugar combo underneath the pie shell, the result is a crisp, sweet crust topped with an earthy, smooth pumpkin filling. It really works.

1 flaky pastry crust recipe for a single crust (see page 35)

1 (15-oz.) can pumpkin puree

1 (12-oz.) can evaporated milk

2 eggs, lightly beaten

½ cup sugar

½ teaspoon salt

1 teaspoon cinnamon

¼ teaspoon ground ginger

¼ teaspoon ground nutmeg

1 tablespoon butter

1 tablespoon light brown sugar

1. Preheat the oven to 400 degrees.

2. In a large bowl, combine the pumpkin puree, evaporated milk, eggs, sugar, salt, cinnamon, ginger, and nutmeg. Stir to combine thoroughly.

3. Put the skillet over medium heat and melt the butter in it. Add the brown sugar and cook, stirring constantly, until sugar is dissolved, 1 or 2 minutes. Carefully remove pan from heat.

4. Place the piecrust over the sugar mixture. Fill with the pumpkin mix.

5. Put the skillet in the oven and bake for 15 minutes, then reduce the heat to 325 degrees and bake an additional 30 to 45 minutes until the filling is firm and a toothpick inserted in the middle comes out clean. Don't overcook.

6. Allow to cool before serving. Serve with fresh whipped cream.

MAPLE PUMPKIN PIE

SERVES 6 TO 8 ✦ **ACTIVE TIME: 30 MINUTES** ✦ **START TO FINISH: 2 HOURS**

Reducing the amount of sugar and adding Grade B (dark) maple syrup creates a pumpkin pie whose flavor is richer and more nuanced than a regular pumpkin pie. Top with a maple-pecan topping for an over-the-top taste!

1 flaky pastry crust recipe for a single crust (see page 35)

1 (15-oz.) can pumpkin puree

1 (12-oz.) can evaporated milk

2 eggs, lightly beaten

¼ cup sugar

¼ cup 100% natural maple syrup (preferably Grade B dark)

½ teaspoon salt

1 teaspoon cinnamon

¼ teaspoon ground ginger

¼ teaspoon ground nutmeg

1 tablespoon butter

1 tablespoon light brown sugar

Topping

1½ cups pecan pieces

4 tablespoons butter, melted

4 tablespoons 100% natural maple syrup (preferably Grade B dark)

1. Preheat the oven to 400 degrees.

2. In a large bowl, combine the pumpkin puree, evaporated milk, eggs, sugar, maple syrup, salt, cinnamon, ginger, and nutmeg. Stir to combine thoroughly.

3. Put the skillet over medium heat and melt the butter in it. Add the brown sugar and cook, stirring constantly, until sugar is dissolved, 1 or 2 minutes. Carefully remove pan from heat.

4. Place the piecrust over the sugar mixture. Fill with the pumpkin mix.

5. Put the skillet in the oven and bake for 15 minutes, then reduce the heat to 325 degrees and bake an additional 30 to 45 minutes until the filling is firm and a toothpick inserted in the middle comes out clean. Don't overcook.

6. Make the maple-pecan topping by putting the pecan pieces, butter, and maple syrup in a bowl and stirring to thoroughly combine. Spoon the mixture and carefully spread over the top of the pie. Preheat the broiler to high. Place an oven rack on the top shelf. Broil the pie until the topping is just toasted, keeping an eye on it to be sure it doesn't burn, about 5 minutes. Cool slightly before serving.

CUSTARD & CREAM PIES

These are some of the yummiest pies going, as they
tend to be fluffy and gooey. There's a great variety of
custard and cream pies in this chapter, and all are built
on crusts that complement their flavors. They're fun,
too, and some of the tastiest combinations involve crusts
made with everything from cookies to nuts. Many of
them don't require baking, either, which makes them
especially enjoyable in summer when you don't want to
turn the oven on. So dig in and see which ones become
your favorites!

CHOCOLATE PUDDING PIE

SERVES 6 TO 8 ✦ ACTIVE TIME: 20 MINUTES ✦ START TO FINISH: 90 MINUTES

Whatever you do, don't skip adding the whipped topping on this pie. It truly is the "secret ingredient" that brings it all together. Garnishing with fresh raspberries or strawberry pieces adds flavor and color.

1 graham cracker crust (see page 40)

2 (3.5-oz.) boxes instant chocolate pudding (dark chocolate is preferable)

3 cups whole milk

2 cups whipped topping (Cool Whip or fresh whipped cream)

Whole fresh raspberries or sliced strawberries for garnish (if desired)

1. In a large bowl, combine the pudding mix and milk. Whisk until all the lumps are broken up, the pudding is smooth, and it has started to thicken, about 5 minutes.

2. Put the pudding in the graham cracker crust and cover with plastic wrap. Refrigerate for an hour or longer.

3. Before serving, top with the whipped topping and garnish with the fruit, if desired.

VANILLA– BUTTERSCOTCH PUDDING PIE

SERVES 6 TO 8 ✦ ACTIVE TIME: 40 MINUTES ✦ START TO FINISH: 2 HOURS

The layers in this pie are fashioned from the two flavors of pudding. The result is a pie that's as pleasing to the eye as it is to the tummy. Sprinkle with mini chocolate morsels for an extra treat.

1 graham cracker crust (see page 40)

1 (3.5-oz.) box instant vanilla pudding

1 (3.5-oz.) box instant butterscotch pudding

3 cups whole milk

½ cup semisweet chocolate mini morsels (if desired), or finely chopped white chocolate pieces

1. In a medium bowl, combine the vanilla pudding mix and 1½ cups milk. Whisk until all the lumps are broken up, the pudding is smooth, and it has started to thicken, about 5 minutes.

2. Put the pudding in the graham cracker crust and refrigerate.

3. In another bowl, combine the butterscotch pudding mix and 1½ cups milk. Whisk until all the lumps are broken up, the pudding is smooth, and it has started to thicken, about 5 minutes.

4. Gently spread the butterscotch pudding over the vanilla pudding to form a second layer and cover with plastic wrap. Refrigerate for an hour or longer.

5. Before serving, sprinkle with the chocolate morsels or pieces.

PECAN-MAPLE CREAM PIE

**SERVES 6 TO 8 ✦ ACTIVE TIME: 60 MINUTES ✦
START TO FINISH: SEVERAL HOURS OR OVERNIGHT**

*A word of warning: leave the calorie counting behind when you bite into this pie. It is
a sinfully delicious sugar-cream confection whose pecan crust sets the stage for the billowy,
smooth sweetness of the filling. Drizzled with maple caramel, it's a home run.*

1 pecan nut crust
(see page 44)

2 cups 100% natural
maple syrup (preferably
Grade B dark)

1 cup heavy cream

Pinch of salt

½ cup cornstarch

½ cup water

Maple Caramel Sauce

8 tablespoons butter

1 cup light brown sugar

¼ teaspoon salt

1 cup 100% natural
maple syrup (preferably
Grade B dark)

1. In a heavy-bottomed saucepan over medium-high heat, combine the maple syrup, and heavy cream. Stir, cooking, until mixture is heated through and boiling. Reduce the heat to medium low and let simmer for about 5 minutes, stirring occasionally. Add the salt and remove from the heat.

2. In a measuring cup, combine the cornstarch and water and stir to combine thoroughly.

3. Return the saucepan to medium-low heat and stir in the cornstarch/water mix. Cook, stirring, until mixture thickens, about 8 to 10 minutes. Allow to cool slightly before pouring into the pie crust and spreading evenly. Cover with plastic wrap and refrigerate for several hours or overnight.

4. About a half hour before serving, make the maple caramel sauce. Melt the butter over medium heat in a saucepan. Stir in the brown sugar and salt and cook, stirring, until sauce starts to boil. Keep stirring as the sauce boils, about 3 minutes. Stir in maple syrup and continue to stir while the sauce boils, another 2 to 3 minutes. Remove from heat and cool slightly.

5. When ready to serve the pie, drizzle the caramel over it in a decorative pattern. Serve extra sauce on the side. Leftover sauce can be stored in a sealed jar in the refrigerator for several months.

CHOCOLATE SALTED-PISTACHIO PUDDING PIE

SERVES 6 TO 8 ✦ ACTIVE TIME: 60 MINUTES ✦ START TO FINISH: 2 HOURS

So easy to make and so good! And so colorful, too. Kids love this one. And guess what? So do adults. It'll become a go-to recipe.

1 tablespoon butter

8 ounces vanilla wafer cookies, crushed

6 tablespoons butter, melted

2 ounces semisweet baking chocolate

¼ cup sweetened condensed milk

1 cup salted, shelled pistachio pieces, divided

2 (3.4-oz.) boxes instant pistachio pudding mix

2 cups milk

1 cup whipped topping (Cool Whip or fresh whipped cream), if desired

1. Melt the tablespoon of butter in the cast-iron skillet over low heat.

2. In a large bowl, mix the cookie crumbs with the 6 tablespoons butter until combined. Carefully remove the cast-iron skillet from the heat and press the cookie mixture into the bottom of the pan to form a crust. Allow to cool and set.

3. In a small microwave-safe bowl, melt the chocolate in 15-second increments, stirring after each, until just melted. Stir in the sweetened condensed milk.

4. Pour the chocolate mixture over the pie crust. Sprinkle with half of the salted pistachio pieces. Refrigerate for about 30 minutes.

5. In a large bowl, whisk together the pudding mix and milk for about 3 minutes, until smooth and thickened. Put the pudding into the crust and spread evenly. Sprinkle with remaining pistachios. Add a layer of whipped topping, if desired.

6. Cover with plastic wrap and refrigerate for at least 1 hour and up to 1 day. When ready to serve, remove plastic wrap and sprinkle with additional salted pistachio pieces.

BANANA PUDDING PIE

SERVES 6 TO 8 ✦ ACTIVE TIME: 45 MINUTES ✦ START TO FINISH: SEVERAL HOURS

You can go several ways with this pie and end up with something really tasty in all instances. One is to use instant vanilla pudding and top the pie with banana slices. Another is to use banana-flavored instant pudding, to which you could stir in some whipped topping for a lighter texture, and top with sliced bananas. The third is the recipe given here. It's made with pudding, made from scratch, flavored with real bananas—and topped with banana slices! It's the winner, for sure.

1 graham cracker crust
(see page 40)

1 cup whole milk

1 cup heavy cream

2 large bananas,
very ripe, sliced thin

3 tablespoons
cornstarch

3 egg yolks

⅓ cup 100% natural
maple syrup (preferably
Grade B dark)
or ½ cup sugar

1 teaspoon vanilla

Dash of salt

1 medium banana,
just ripe, sliced into
¼-inch pieces

1. In a small saucepan over medium-high heat, stir together the milk and heavy cream. Cook, stirring constantly, until heated through. Gently add the banana slices, reduce the heat to low, and use a fork to mash the milk and fruit together. Continue to cook over low heat, stirring occasionally, until the mixture is hot but not boiling. Slowly stir in the cornstarch, 1 tablespoon at a time.

2. Keep the milk mixture on very low heat. In another bowl, beat the egg yolks until they're combined. Stir in the maple syrup. Add a large spoonful of the hot milk mix to the yolks and whisk briskly to combine. Do this 2 more times until you've put about ½ cup of hot milk into the yolk mixture.

3. Next, gently whisk the yolk mixture into the saucepan with the rest of the milk/cream/banana mix. Slowly bring the mixture to a gentle boil and while stirring constantly, boil for a couple of minutes. Remove from heat and stir in the vanilla and a pinch of salt.

4. Allow the mixture to cool, then pour it into the pie crust. Top with sliced bananas, cover with plastic wrap, and refrigerate for several hours before serving.

LEMON RICE PUDDING PIE

SERVES 6 TO 8 ✦ ACTIVE TIME: 30 MINUTES ✦ START TO FINISH: 3 OR MORE HOURS

I had leftover rice one night and I thought that the rice would be a nice texture and flavor addition to a pudding pie. I chose lemon for the filling and enhanced the flavor with some fresh squeezed lemon juice and vanilla extract. This is now a family favorite.

1 graham cracker crust (see page 40)

1 (3.4-oz.) box instant lemon pudding mix

2 cups whole milk

1 tablespoon fresh squeezed lemon juice

1 teaspoon vanilla extract

1½ to 2 cups cooked rice (brown rice is best)

1 cup whipped topping (Cool Whip or fresh whipped cream)

Cinnamon (optional)

1. In a large bowl, combine the lemon pudding mix and milk. Whisk until all the lumps are broken up, the pudding is smooth, and it has started to thicken, about 3 minutes. Stir in the lemon juice and vanilla, then stir in the rice.

2. Put the filling into the pie crust. Put a piece of plastic wrap over it, covering the filling, and refrigerate for 2 or more hours before serving.

3. Top with the whipped topping and sprinkle with cinnamon, if desired.

PIÑA COLADA PUDDING PIE

SERVES 6 TO 8 ✦ ACTIVE TIME: 45 MINUTES ✦ START TO FINISH: SEVERAL HOURS

Seriously, piña colada pie. If you think it sounds temptingly weird, you're right. If you love a good piña colada with its combo of fresh coconut and sweet pineapple, you're going to love this pie. It really is a cocktail in a crust.

1 baked crust
(see page 32)

½ cup unsweetened
coconut flakes

1 (3.4-oz.) box instant
coconut pudding mix

1 cup milk

1 cup piña colada mix
(non-alcoholic)

¼ cup dark rum

2 tablespoons
cornstarch

Kiwi slices, pineapple
slices, and coconut
shavings for garnish
(optional)

1. Sprinkle the unsweetened coconut flakes in the bottom of the baked pie crust and set aside.

2. In a large bowl, combine the coconut pudding mix with the milk and piña colada mix. Whisk until all the lumps are broken up, the pudding is smooth, and it has started to thicken, about 3 minutes.

3. In a small saucepan, heat the rum over a low flame. When it's warm, add the cornstarch and stir with a fork or a small whisk until it is completely blended and warmed throughout. Remove from heat and continue to stir while allowing the mixture to cool slightly.

4. Add the rum mixture to the pudding and stir gently to combine.

5. Pour the filling into the baked pie crust. Cover with plastic wrap, press the plastic into the filling, and refrigerate for several hours before serving. Garnish as desired.

BANANA CREAM PIE

SERVES 6 TO 8 ✦ ACTIVE TIME: 30 MINUTES ✦ START TO FINISH: 6+ HOURS

This is simply a more decadent version of the banana pudding pie, as it is made from scratch and is built in layers. Be prepared for the whole thing to be eaten in one sitting!

1 baked crust
(see page 32)

1 cup sugar

¼ cup cornstarch

½ teaspoon salt

3 cups milk

2 eggs

3 tablespoons butter,
cut into smaller pieces

1½ teaspoons vanilla

2 large bananas,
not overly ripened

1 cup whipped topping
(Cool Whip or fresh
whipped cream)

1. In a large saucepan, combine sugar, cornstarch, salt, and milk and whisk together until smooth. Cook over medium heat, stirring continuously, until thickened and just starting to boil, about 7 minutes. Reduce heat; cook and stir 2 minutes longer. Remove from heat.

2. In a small bowl, stir the eggs together until combined. Add a scoop of the hot custard, stirring briskly so the eggs don't congeal or cook. When the hot custard is completely combined with the eggs, stir the egg mixture into the saucepan of custard.

3. With the saucepan on a medium heat, cook, stirring constantly, until the mixture comes to a gentle boil, and continue to stir and cook for about 2 minutes. Remove from heat and stir in butter and vanilla. Cover with plastic wrap, pressing it onto the custard. Refrigerate for at least 30 minutes.

4. Spread half of the custard into the baked pie crust. Slice bananas; arrange over filling. Pour remaining custard over bananas. Spread with whipped topping.

5. Refrigerate at least 6 hours before serving.

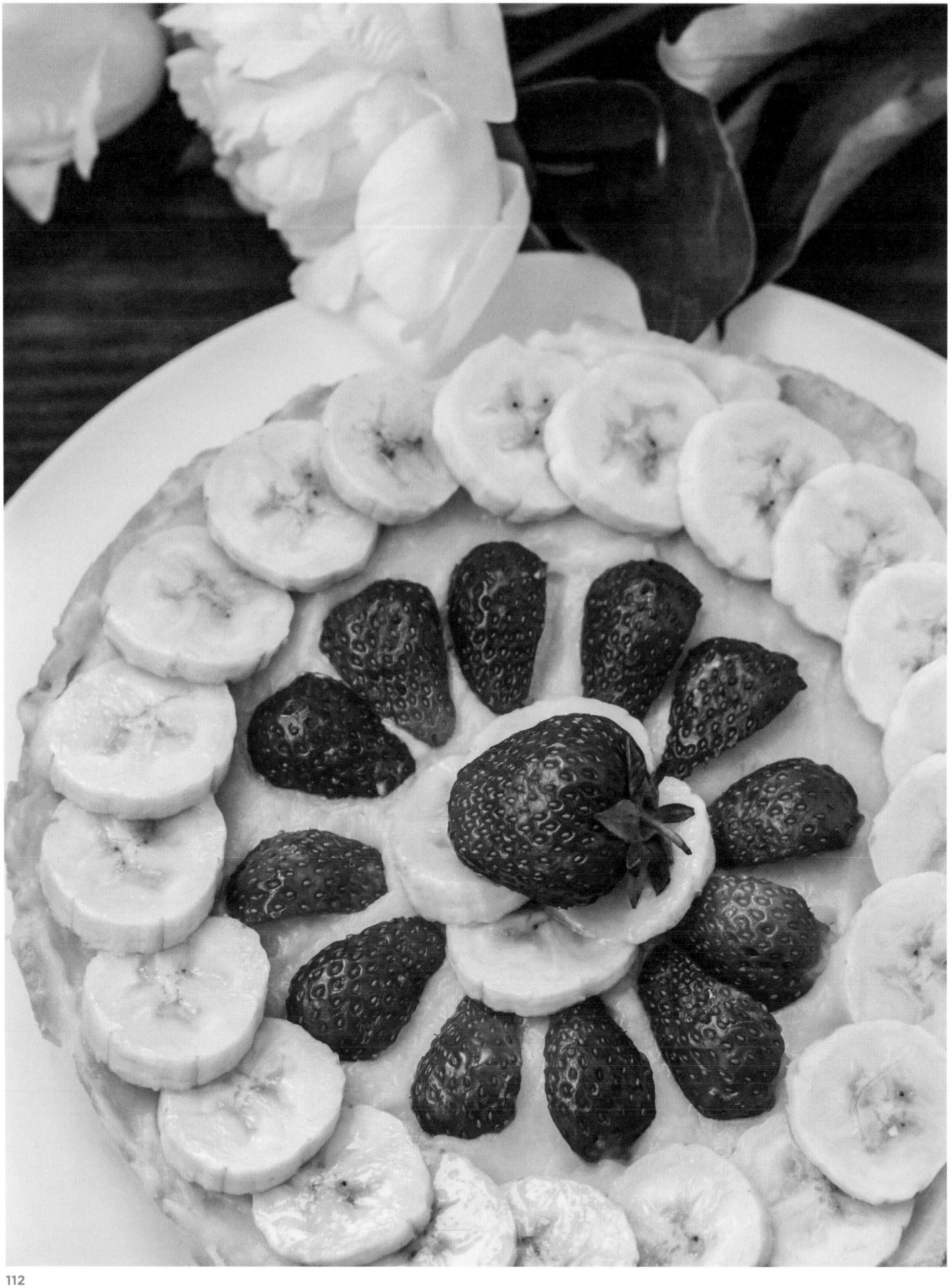

BANANA-STRAWBERRY CREAM PIE

**SERVES 6 TO 8 ✦ ACTIVE TIME: 1 HOUR ✦
START TO FINISH: SEVERAL HOURS OR OVERNIGHT**

My mother always reminded me that if something came out looking not-so-great, it didn't matter as long as it tasted really good. I can say that this pie will always taste really good no matter how it comes out for you, but when it works and the banana layer settles on the crust and the pink filling sets on top of it, it is as beautiful as it is delicious. The gelatin in this recipe produces a very smooth cream filling.

1 baked crust
(see page 32)

½ cup sugar, divided

Pinch of salt

1 envelope
unflavored gelatin
(about 1 tablespoon)

3 eggs, separated

1¼ cups milk

1 teaspoon vanilla
extract

¾ cup heavy cream

1 cup sliced
strawberries, cut into
dime-sized pieces

1-2 bananas, just ripe

Whole strawberries
for garnish

Chocolate sauce
to drizzle, if desired

1. In a small saucepan, stir together ¼ cup of the sugar, salt, and gelatin.

2. In a bowl, whisk together the egg yolks with the milk. Add the egg and milk mixture to the saucepan and stir to combine thoroughly. Over medium-low heat, cook, stirring constantly, as mixture warms and thickens. Do not bring to a boil. Cook until the mixture coats the back of a spoon. Remove from heat and stir in the vanilla and heavy cream. When slightly cooler, put the saucepan in the refrigerator to cool and further thicken the mixture, about 45 minutes.

3. In a large bowl, beat the egg whites with an electric mixer, working the rest of the sugar gradually into the whites as they're beaten until they stiffen and the sugar is dissolved.

4. Take the saucepan out of the refrigerator and whisk the cold custard until it's smooth. Fold it into the beaten egg whites. Stir in the strawberry pieces.

5. Slice the banana into ¼-inch slices and place in a single layer on top of the pie crust. Pour the strawberry cream filling over the banana slices and spread evenly. Cover with plastic wrap and refrigerate for several hours or up to 1 day before serving.

6. When ready to serve, remove plastic wrap and garnish with whole strawberries. Drizzle with chocolate sauce if desired.

PINEAPPLE CREAM PIE

This creamy pie has the great zing of pineapple, plus it's really fun to decorate with the pineapple rings and maraschino cherries. The result is a taste of the tropics with a modern take on pineapple upside down cake.

1 baked crust
(see page 32)

½ cup sugar

3 tablespoons
cornstarch

¼ teaspoon salt

1¾ cup milk

¾ cup pineapple juice
from a can of sliced
pineapple rings

3 egg yolks

1 tablespoon butter

1 (20-oz.) can pineapple
rings

Maraschino cherries

1. In a medium saucepan, combine sugar, cornstarch, and salt. Whisk to combine. Stir in the milk until smooth. Cook over medium-low heat, stirring constantly, until mixture begins to thicken and just begins to boil. Don't allow to boil. Add the pineapple juice and continue to stir until thoroughly combined. Remove from the heat.

2. In a small bowl, whisk egg yolks. Add a large spoonful of the pineapple cream and stir rapidly to prevent curdling or cooking. Repeat, being sure to stir rapidly. Next, stir the egg mixture into the saucepan with the pineapple cream, and stir that briskly to combine. Return saucepan to low heat, and stir in the butter. Continue to stir while cooking, until mixture thickens considerably, about 5 minutes.

3. Pour into pie crust and spread evenly. Cover with plastic wrap and refrigerate several hours or up to 1 day.

4. When ready to serve, remove plastic wrap and decorate with pineapple rings, putting cherries in the centers of the rings or as desired.

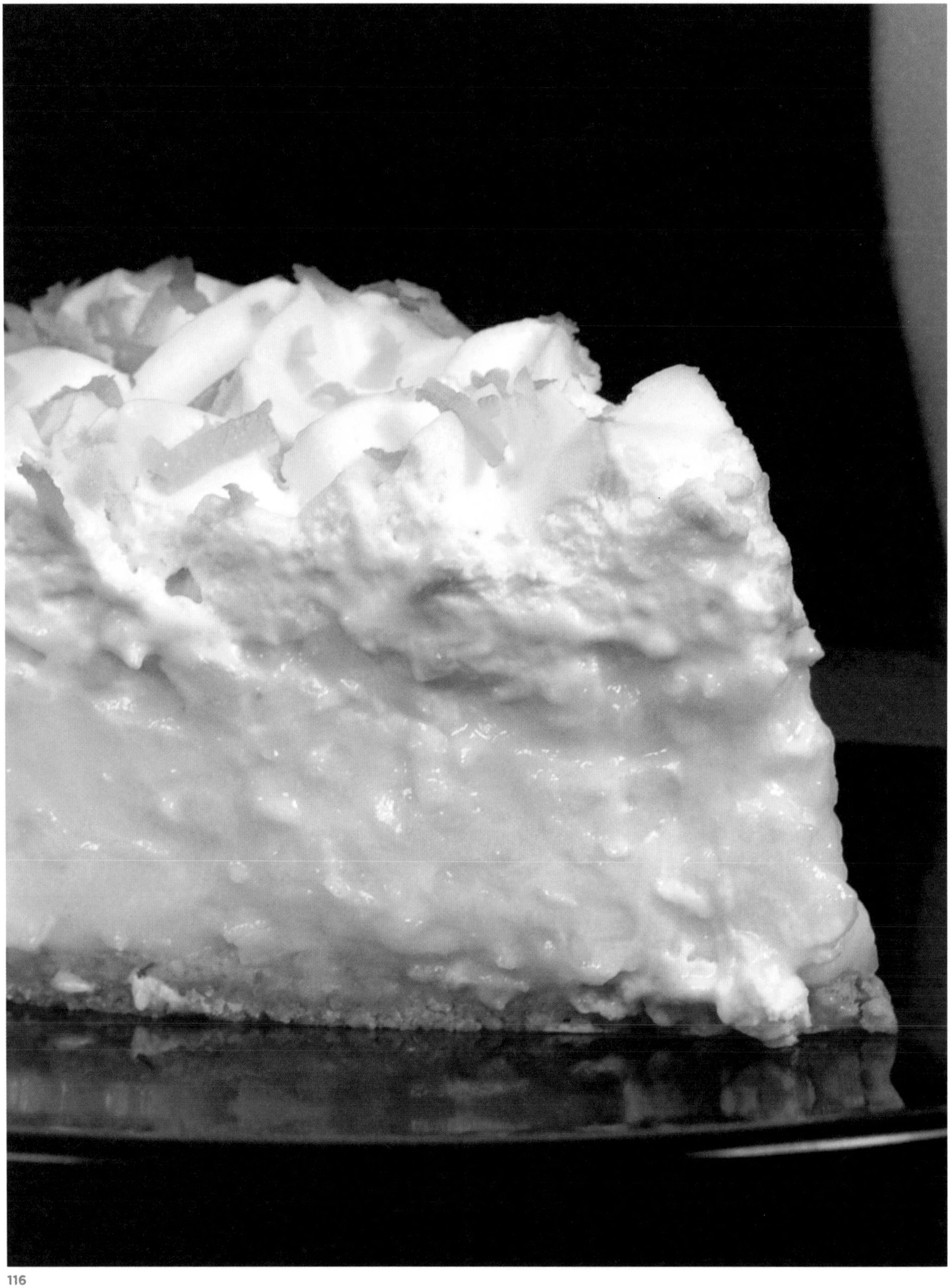

COCONUT CREAM PIE

SERVES 6 TO 8 ✦ ACTIVE TIME: 60 MINUTES ✦ START TO FINISH: 2 OR MORE HOURS

Make this pie on a cold day if you want to feel like you're taking a vacation in the tropics. Make it on a warm day if you just love the taste of coconut and all the beach associations it brings with it. Make it any time, because it's really good.

1 baked crust
(see page 32)

1 cup sugar

¼ cup cornstarch

½ teaspoon salt

3 cups milk

2 eggs

3 tablespoons butter,
cut into smaller pieces

1 teaspoons vanilla

½ teaspoon coconut
extract or coconut rum

1½ cups unsweetened
coconut flakes

1. In a large saucepan, combine sugar, cornstarch, salt, and milk and whisk together until smooth. Cook over medium heat, stirring continuously, until thickened and just starting to boil, about 7 minutes. Reduce heat; cook and stir 2 minutes longer. Remove from heat.

2. In a small bowl, stir the eggs together until combined. Add a scoop of the hot custard, stirring briskly so the eggs don't congeal or cook. When the hot custard is completely combined with the eggs, stir the egg mixture into the saucepan of custard.

3. With the saucepan on medium heat, cook, stirring constantly, until the mixture comes to a gentle boil, and continue to stir and cook for about 2 minutes. Remove from heat and stir in butter, vanilla, and coconut extract or rum. Gently fold in the unsweetened coconut, stirring just to combine. Cover with plastic wrap, pressing it onto the custard. Refrigerate for at least 30 minutes.

4. Fill the baked pie crust with the pudding, cover with plastic wrap again, and refrigerate for at least an hour before serving.

CHOCOLATE-ESPRESSO CREAM PIE

**SERVES 6 TO 8 ✦ ACTIVE TIME: 45 MINUTES ✦
START TO FINISH: SEVERAL HOURS OR OVERNIGHT**

For those of us who love the combination of chocolate and coffee flavors, this pie is a winner. The espresso adds an earthiness and additional layer of flavor that is rich and satisfying. I like to use an almond crust for this pie, but if that seems like too much, use a baked crust instead.

1 chocolate graham cracker crust (see page 40)

3½ cups heavy cream

1 (11.5-oz.) bag of semisweet chocolate morsels

1 teaspoon vanilla extract

1 tablespoon instant espresso powder or coffee

Pinch of salt

½ cup toasted almond pieces (optional)

1. In a heavy-bottomed saucepan, heat 2 cups heavy cream over medium heat until heated through. Stir in the chocolate morsels and stir until melted. Add the vanilla, espresso powder, and pinch of salt, and continue to stir until thoroughly combined. Remove from heat and set aside.

2. In a large bowl, beat 1½ cups cream with an electric mixer until it forms stiff peaks, Fold the whipped cream into the chocolate-espresso mixture. Transfer the filling to the pie crust, spreading evenly to fill. Cover with plastic wrap and refrigerate for at least 1 hour and up to 1 day.

3. Top with toasted almond pieces if desired.

NUTTY BUTTERSCOTCH PIE

**SERVES 6 TO 8 ✦ ACTIVE TIME: 60 MINUTES ✦
START TO FINISH: SEVERAL HOURS OR OVERNIGHT**

Making a crust of mixed nuts for this pie brings out all kinds of nutty notes in the butterscotch filling. This is extreme comfort food. Serve with a glass of sherry or port for an extra-special treat.

1 mixed nut crust
(see page 44)

½ cup (8 tablespoons)
butter

1¼ cups light brown
sugar

1½ cups hot water

¼ cup cornstarch

3 tablespoons flour

½ teaspoon salt

1½ cups heavy cream

½ cup whole milk

4 egg yolks

1 teaspoon vanilla
extract

1 cup toasted pecan
pieces

1. In a saucepan over medium heat, melt the butter until it just starts to brown. Add the brown sugar and hot water and whisk to combine. Cook, whisking or stirring, until the mixture just comes to a boil. Remove from heat and set aside.

2. In a small bowl, stir together the cornstarch, flour, and salt. Add ½ cup of the cream and stir to combine and remove lumps. Stir in remaining cup of cream and the milk until thoroughly combined. Add this to the butter mixture, whisking briskly to combine without curdling. Replace over the heat and stir until the mixture thickens, about 3 minutes.

3. In a separate small bowl, whisk the egg yolks until combined. Add a large spoonful of the hot cream mixture, whisking briskly. Repeat, and then add the egg mixture to the cream mixture, whisking to combine all. Return to medium heat and cook, stirring or whisking, for another minute. Remove from heat and add the vanilla.

4. Pour into the pie crust and distribute evenly. Cover with plastic wrap and refrigerate for several hours or up to 1 day. When ready to serve, remove the plastic wrap and sprinkle with the toasted pecans.

IRISH CREAM PIE

SERVES 6 TO 8 ✦ ACTIVE TIME: 60 MINUTES ✦
START TO FINISH: SEVERAL HOURS OR OVERNIGHT

I think we can all remember our first glass of Irish Cream liqueur and how good it tasted and how easily it went down. It's positively addicting! This pie is a celebration of that goodness. You'll be asking for seconds, for sure!

1 chocolate graham cracker crust (see page 40) or a baked crust (see page 32)

1 (11-oz.) bag white chocolate morsels

⅓ cup Irish Cream liqueur

4 large egg whites

¼ cup sugar

1 cup heavy cream

1 teaspoon unsweetened cocoa powder (optional)

1. Mix chocolate morsels and liqueur in a metal bowl. Place it over a pot of simmering water and melt the chocolate with the cream, stirring occasionally until combined and smooth.

2. In a separate large bowl, beat the egg whites with an electric mixer on high until soft peaks form. Add the sugar by tablespoons, beating until dissolved between additions, and until stiff peaks form.

3. Clean the beaters and, in another bowl, beat the heavy cream until stiff. Fold the whipped cream and egg whites together, and then gently fold in the chocolate mixture.

4. Pour into the pie crust and distribute evenly. Cover with plastic wrap and refrigerate for 3 hours or up to 1 day before serving. If desired, lightly sprinkle with unsweetened cocoa powder.

LEMON BRÛLÉE PIE

SERVES 6 TO 8 ✦ ACTIVE TIME: 30 MINUTES ✦ START TO FINISH: 2 HOURS

Another zinger of a lemon pie, loaded with fresh lemon juice and heavy cream, two nearly perfect foods. As this pie bakes in the oven for nearly an hour, it fills your home with its lemony goodness. Delicious in every way.

1 baked crust
(see page 32)

6 eggs

1¼ cup sugar

zest from 2 lemons

¾ cup fresh squeezed
lemon juice (don't use
bottled lemon juice)

2 teaspoons lemon
liqueur (optional but
worth it)

⅔ cup heavy cream

1. Preheat the oven to 300 degrees.

2. In a large bowl, beat the eggs until just combined. Add the sugar, zest, lemon juice and lemon liqueur, and whisk or stir until well combined and sugar is dissolved.

3. Stir in heavy cream.

4. Fill pie crust with lemon/cream mixture, tapping to distribute filling evenly.

5. Bake for 50 to 60 minutes, testing after 50 minutes to see if center is set. If it is, remove from oven. If it's still runny, continue baking, testing after another 5 minutes, etc., until set in center.

6. Allow to cool before serving.

CHOCOLATE MOUSSE PIE

**SERVES 6 TO 8 ✦ ACTIVE TIME: 45 MINUTES ✦
START TO FINISH: SEVERAL HOURS OR OVERNIGHT**

Doesn't this sound amazingly good? The secret is the darkness and richness of the chocolate filling, which is why it's made with heavy cream and dark chocolate morsels. You can change this one up, too, by making different kinds of cookie crusts or by using a nut crust, instead (hazelnut would be wonderful).

1 chocolate graham cracker crust (see page 40)

4 cups heavy cream

1 (10-oz.) bag of dark chocolate morsels

2 cups mini marshmallows

1 teaspoon vanilla extract

Pinch of salt

¼ cup confectioners' sugar

2 tablespoons unsweetened cocoa powder

1. In a heavy-bottomed saucepan, heat 2 cups heavy cream over medium heat until heated through. Stir in the chocolate morsels and stir until melted. Add the marshmallows, vanilla, and pinch of salt, and continue to stir until marshmallows are melted and combined. Remove from heat and set aside.

2. In a large bowl, beat 1 cup cream with an electric mixer until it forms stiff peaks. Fold the whipped cream into the chocolate mixture. Transfer chocolate filling to the pie crust, spreading evenly to fill. Cover with plastic wrap and refrigerate for at least 1 hour and up to 1 day.

3. Before serving, beat remaining 1 cup of heavy cream in a bowl with an electric mixer. As the cream stiffens, add the confectioners' sugar and cocoa powder. Continue to beat until stiff peaks form.

4. Remove pie from refrigerator and top with the whipped cream. Serve.

LEMON MERINGUE PIE

SERVES 6 TO 8 ✦ ACTIVE TIME: 60 MINUTES ✦ START TO FINISH: 90 MINUTES

This is one of my very favorite pies, and there are several ways you can make it. They all taste great. This is the first of three recipes. Be sure to use fresh squeezed lemon juice, not the juice that's already pressed. It makes a huge difference.

1 baked crust (see page 32)

⅓ cup cornstarch

1 cup sugar

Pinch of salt

1½ cups water

Grated peel of 1 lemon

½ cup fresh squeezed lemon juice (no seeds)

4 eggs, separated

1 tablespoon butter

¼ teaspoon salt

½ cup sugar

1. Preheat the oven to 400 degrees.

2. In a saucepan, combine cornstarch, sugar, and pinch of salt. Whisk to combine. Stir in the water, lemon peel, and lemon juice. Cook over medium heat, stirring constantly until mixture comes to a boil. Remove from heat.

3. In the bowl with the egg yolks, add a spoonful of the hot lemon mixture. Stir rapidly to combine so the eggs don't cook or curdle. Add another spoonful of the lemon mix and repeat. Transfer the egg yolk mixture to the saucepan with the lemon mixture and stir constantly to combine well.

4. Over medium heat, continue to stir and add the butter. Stir until butter is completely melted and blended and the mixture has thickened, about 3 minutes.

5. Pour filling into the pie crust.

6. In a large bowl, beat the egg whites and the salt with an electric mixer on high until soft peaks form. Continue to beat, adding 2 tablespoons of sugar at a time until the sugar is dissolved. Work in increments of 2 tablespoons until all the sugar has been beaten in and the egg whites have formed stiff peaks.

7. Spoon onto the lemon filling and spread to cover evenly.

8. Put the skillet in the oven for about 10 minutes until the meringue is just golden.

9. Allow to cool completely before serving.

QUICK AND EASY LEMON MERINGUE PIE

SERVES 6 TO 8 ✦ ACTIVE TIME: 45 MINUTES ✦ START TO FINISH: 2 OR MORE HOURS

This is a very tasty lemon meringue pie you can make much more quickly and easily than the other. Enhance the flavor if you can by adding fresh squeezed lemon juice, but if you don't have it or don't want to, it'll still taste great. The graham cracker crust adds texture and flavor.

1 graham cracker crust (see page 40)

1 (3.4-oz.) box instant lemon pudding mix

2 cups whole milk

2 tablespoons fresh squeezed lemon juice (optional)

3 egg whites

Pinch of salt

¼ cup sugar

1. In a medium bowl, combine the lemon pudding mix with the milk. Whisk until all the lumps are broken up, the pudding is smooth, and it has started to thicken, about 3 minutes. Add lemon juice if desired. Set aside.

2. Make the meringue. In a large bowl, beat the egg whites and the salt with an electric mixer on high until soft peaks form. Continue to beat, adding 2 tablespoons of sugar at a time until the sugar is dissolved. Work in increments of 2 tablespoons until all the sugar has been beaten in and the egg whites have formed stiff peaks.

3. Gently fold the pudding into the meringue until combined. Pour into the pie crust.

4. Cover with plastic wrap and refrigerate for at least 1 hour and up to 1 day. Serve.

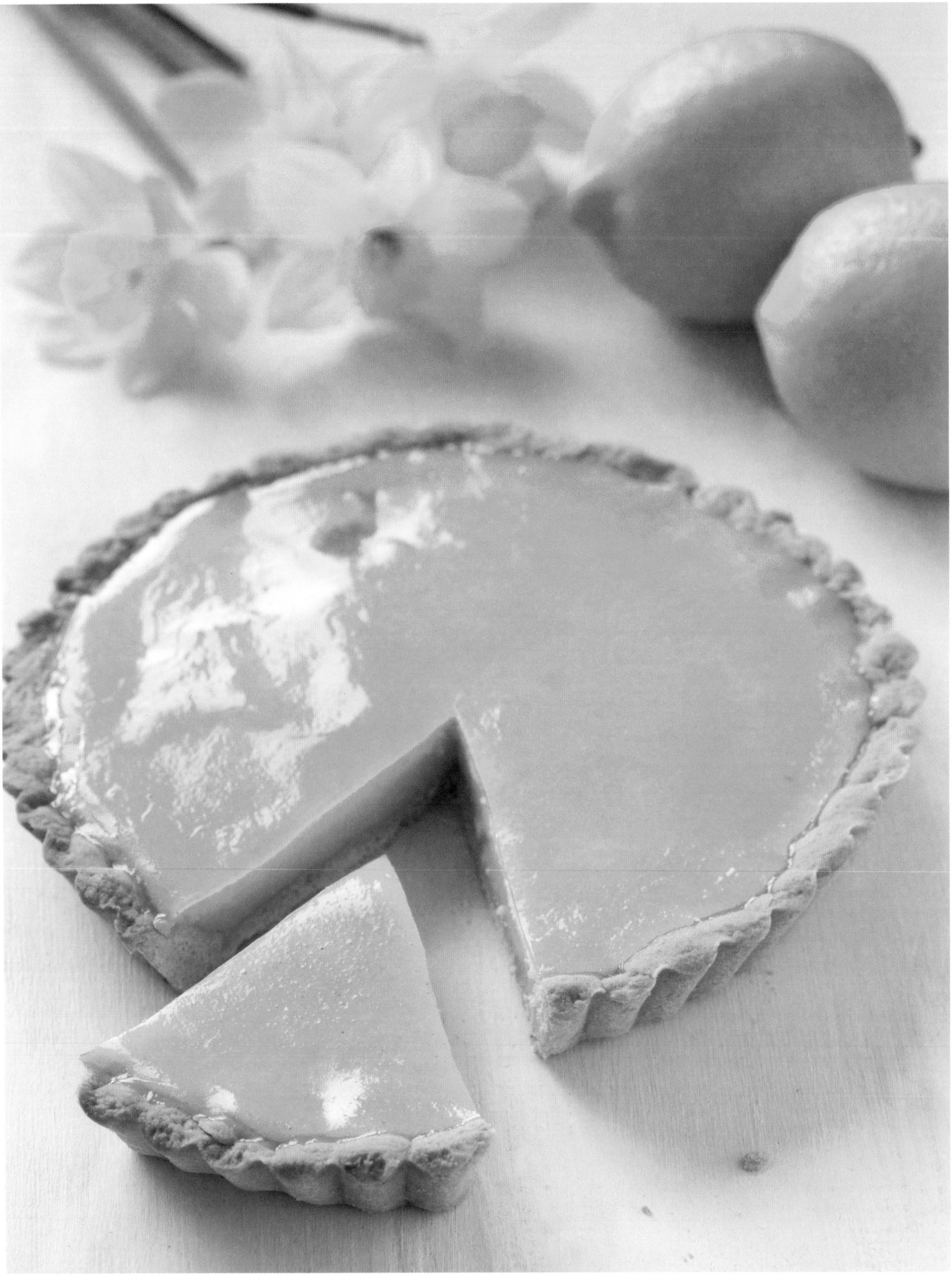

UPSIDE DOWN LEMON MERINGUE PIE

SERVES 6 TO 8 ✦ ACTIVE TIME: 60 MINUTES ✦
START TO FINISH: SEVERAL HOURS OR OVERNIGHT

This one is called "upside down lemon meringue pie," because the meringue is the crust! Just be sure the lemon filling is completely cool before putting it in the crust or the meringue will melt.

1 meringue crust (see page 43)

⅓ cup cornstarch

1 cup sugar

Pinch of salt

1½ cups water

Grated peel of 1 lemon

½ cup fresh squeezed lemon juice (no seeds)

4 egg yolks

1 tablespoon butter

1. In a saucepan, combine cornstarch, sugar, and pinch of salt. Whisk to combine. Stir in the water, lemon peel, and lemon juice. Cook over medium heat, stirring constantly until mixture comes to a boil. Remove from heat.

2. In the bowl with the egg yolks, add a spoonful of the hot lemon mixture. Stir rapidly to combine so the eggs don't cook or curdle. Add another spoonful of the lemon mix and repeat. Transfer the egg yolk mixture to the saucepan with the lemon mixture and stir constantly to combine well.

3. Over medium heat, continue to stir and add the butter. Stir until butter is completely melted and blended and the mixture has thickened, about 3 minutes. Allow lemon filling to cool completely in the uncovered saucepan, stirring occasionally, about 30 minutes.

4. Pour lemon filling into meringue crust. Cover with plastic wrap and refrigerate for at least 1 hour and up to 1 day before serving.

KEY LIME CHIFFON PIE

SERVES 6 TO 8 ✦ ACTIVE TIME: 30 MINUTES ✦ START TO FINISH: 2 HOURS

This is a fluffier version of a classic key lime pie. What I love about this one is the cloud-like consistency of the filling, which is the perfect complement to the tangy taste of the lime. Don't omit the lime zest from this recipe.

1 graham cracker crust (see page 40)

2 cups heavy cream

¼ cup sugar

⅓ cup fresh squeezed lime juice

Zest from 2 limes

1 envelope (about 1 tablespoon) unflavored gelatin

½ cup sweetened condensed milk

Whipped cream and lime zest or wheels for garnish

1. In a large bowl, beat the cream on high until peaks just start to form. Add the sugar and continue to beat on high until stiff peaks form.

2. In a small saucepan, combine the lime juice, zest, and gelatin, and stir until gelatin is dissolved. Turn the heat on to medium and cook the mixture until it begins to thicken, stirring constantly, about 3 to 5 minutes. Do not let it boil or burn. Remove from heat and allow to cool slightly. Stir in the sweetened condensed milk.

3. Fold this mixture into the whipped cream until combined and smooth. Don't overwork it.

4. Pour the filling into the crust. Cover with plastic wrap and refrigerate until set, about 45 minutes (or refrigerate for up to a day).

GLUTEN-FREE GRAPEFRUIT CUSTARD PIE

This came to a dinner party I attended by way of a native Texan. She claimed that the grapefruits that grew in her yard produced something far tastier than what she made for us in New York, and if so, I'm not sure why she ever moved. The pie became an instant favorite of mine. I like it with vanilla ice cream.

1 baked crust
(see page 32)
or gluten-free crust
(see page 36)

2½ cups sugar, divided

½ cup all-purpose
gluten-free flour

4 egg yolks

4 red grapefruits,
peeled, pith removed,
and sections cut in half

2 cups water

1 (16-oz.) can sweetened
condensed milk

1 teaspoon vanilla
extract

Vanilla ice cream

Grapefruit or kiwi slices
for garnish

1. In a small bowl, stir 2 cups sugar and flour until combined. In another bowl, whisk the egg yolks until well combined. Set aside.

2. Place the grapefruit pieces in a saucepan and add the water. Cook over medium heat, stirring constantly, until the water comes to a boil. Add remaining ½ cup sugar and continue to stir while the mixture boils, another 10 or so minutes. The grapefruit sections will fall apart and yield a thick, pulpy mixture.

3. Remove from heat and stir in the sugar/flour mixture. Add the sweetened condensed milk and stir gently to combine.

4. Put a large spoonful of the hot grapefruit mix into the egg yolks and whisk or stir briskly to combine. Repeat, and then transfer the egg yolk mixture to the saucepan and stir to combine all. Return to the heat and bring to a boil, stirring constantly, and cook for about 10 minutes more. Remove from heat and stir in the vanilla.

5. Pour into the pie crust and distribute evenly. Cover with plastic wrap and refrigerate for several hours or up to a day. When ready to serve, remove the plastic wrap and garnish with fruit slices, if desired. Top slices with vanilla ice cream.

YOGURT CUSTARD PIE WITH BLACKBERRY PRESERVES

SERVES 6 TO 8 ◆ ACTIVE TIME: 60 MINUTES
START TO FINISH: SEVERAL HOURS OR OVERNIGHT

If you want a pie that's a bit healthier than the cream-laden desserts featured in this chapter, this one's for you. Greek yogurt is thick and creamy and just a little tart, and makes a delicious, custard-y filling. Put it in a nut crust (you could use any of the ones described on page 44, but I prefer the almond crust), and top with warmed preserves and you have an easy, instant hit.

1 almond crust
(see page 44)

1 cup low-fat plain
Greek yogurt

2 eggs, lightly beaten

¼ cup sugar

3 tablespoons fresh
squeezed lemon juice

1 teaspoon pure vanilla
extract

½ cup warmed
blackberry preserves

Fresh berries for garnish

1. Preheat the oven to 350 degrees.

2. In a large bowl, whisk together the yogurt, eggs, sugar, lemon juice, and vanilla.

3. Pour into the pie crust and distribute evenly.

4. Put the skillet in the oven and bake for 25 minutes, until the filling is just set. A toothpick inserted in the side of the pie will come out clean, but the center can still look slightly undercooked.

5. Allow to cool for 5 to 10 minutes. Heat the preserves in a small saucepan or a microwave-safe bowl. Spread over the yogurt filling, add fruit for garnish, cover with plastic wrap, and refrigerate several hours before serving.

NUT PIES

Ok, you're going to discover that many of these nut pies feature pecans. Hats off to our friends in the south, who've shown the rest of us how versatile and flavorful this nut can be. Naturally, there's loads of information about pecans on the internet, including a site aptly called: I Love Pecans. There I learned that the pecan tree is the only nut tree that grows naturally in North America. Pecans were a dietary staple of Native Americans, who also made a fermented beverage from them. Early settlers discovered the value of this delicious nut as a food for themselves and the rest of the world, and between 1700 and 1800 the trees were planted by many, including George Washington and Thomas Jefferson. Orchards were established along the Gulf Coast, in Louisiana, and all the way into Texas and northern Mexico. The industry thrives to this day, and this chapter gives a nod to the many ways the pecan is one of the best nuts for pie!

PECAN PIE

SERVES 8 TO 10 ✦ ACTIVE TIME: 30 MINUTES ✦ START TO FINISH: 90 MINUTES

This simple dessert of nuts, eggs, sugar, and vanilla is associated with the goodness of the South, and especially Louisiana, but credit for the creation of the pecan pie is partly attributed to the French, who used the newly discovered nut in a dessert in their early days in the territory. It's also been attributed to a founder of Karo corn syrup. I say Merci and Thank You to both! And don't forget to serve with a scoop of vanilla ice cream!

1 flaky pastry crust recipe for a single crust (see page 35)

3 eggs

1 cup dark corn syrup

½ cup sugar

¼ cup butter, melted

1 teaspoon vanilla extract

1 cup pecan halves or broken pieces

1. Preheat the oven to 350 degrees.

2. In a large bowl, whisk the eggs until thoroughly combined. Add the corn syrup, sugar, melted butter, and vanilla. Whisk until combined, and then stir in the pecan pieces.

3. Pour the filling into the pie crust, shaking the skillet gently to distribute evenly.

4. Put the skillet in the oven and bake for about 60 minutes or until a knife inserted toward the middle comes out clean. If the edge of the crust starts to overly brown, remove the skillet from the oven and put tin foil over the exposed crust until the filling is set.

5. Allow to cool to room temperature before serving.

PECAN–WALNUT PIE

SERVES 8 TO 10 ✦ ACTIVE TIME: 30 MINUTES ✦ START TO FINISH: 90 MINUTES

Walnuts are not as sweet as pecans, so this is a great nut pie to make if you're looking for something a bit nuttier and earthier. Making it in a graham cracker crust adds another dimension, and a dark chocolate drizzle on top takes this one over the top.

**1 graham cracker crust (see page 40)
or 1 flaky pastry crust recipe for a single crust (see page 35)**

3 eggs

1 cup dark corn syrup

⅓ cup sugar

¼ cup butter, melted

1 teaspoon vanilla extract

½ cup pecan pieces

½ cup walnut pieces

4 ounces dark chocolate (70% cocoa)

1. Preheat the oven to 350 degrees.

2. In a large bowl, whisk the eggs until thoroughly combined. Add the corn syrup, sugar, melted butter, and vanilla. Whisk until combined, and then stir in the pecan and walnut pieces.

3. Pour the filling into the pie crust, shaking the skillet gently to distribute evenly.

4. Put the skillet in the oven and bake for about 60 minutes or until a knife inserted toward the middle comes out clean. If the edge of the crust starts to overly brown, remove the skillet from the oven and put tin foil over the exposed crust until the filling is set. Allow to cool completely.

5. In a microwave-safe bowl, break the chocolate up into small pieces. Microwave in 15-second increments, stirring after each one, until chocolate is just melted. Use a spoon to drizzle the chocolate on top of the pie. Refrigerate until set.

CHOCOLATE-BOURBON PECAN PIE

SERVES 8 TO 10 ✦ **ACTIVE TIME: 45 MINUTES** ✦ **START TO FINISH: 2 HOURS**

Here's another notch up in the pecan pie department—the addition of bourbon! It goes with pecans the way chocolate goes with peanut butter. If you're looking to make a fancy pecan pie that will have your guests raving about your cooking, this is the one!

1 chocolate graham
cracker crust
(see page 40)

1½ cups chopped
toasted pecans

6 ounces semisweet
chocolate morsels

1 cup dark corn syrup

⅓ cup sugar

½ cup firmly packed
light brown sugar

¼ cup bourbon

4 large eggs

¼ cup butter, melted

2 teaspoons vanilla
extract

½ teaspoon table salt

1. To toast the pecan pieces, preheat the oven to 350 degrees. Spread the pecan pieces on a baking sheet in a single layer. Bake for 6 to 10 minutes, checking to make sure they don't burn. When cool, break into small pieces.

2. Reduce the oven to 325 degrees.

3. Sprinkle toasted pecan pieces and chocolate morsels evenly onto bottom of pie crust.

4. In a saucepan over medium heat, combine the corn syrup, sugar, light brown sugar, and bourbon. Stir to combine and cook, stirring constantly, until mixture just comes to a boil. At that time, remove from heat.

5. In a large bowl, whisk the eggs until thoroughly combined. Add the melted butter, vanilla, and salt, and whisk to combine. Add about ¼ of the hot liquid to the egg mixture, whisking briskly to combine so the eggs don't curdle and cook. When thoroughly combined, continue to add the hot liquid to the egg mixture in small amounts, whisking to combine thoroughly after each addition until all of it is incorporated. Pour the egg/sugar mixture over the nuts and chocolate pieces and shake the skillet gently to distribute evenly.

6. Put the skillet in the oven and bake for about 60 minutes or until a knife inserted toward the middle comes out clean. If the edge of the crust starts to overly brown, remove the skillet from the oven and put tin foil over the exposed crust until the filling is set. Allow to cool completely.

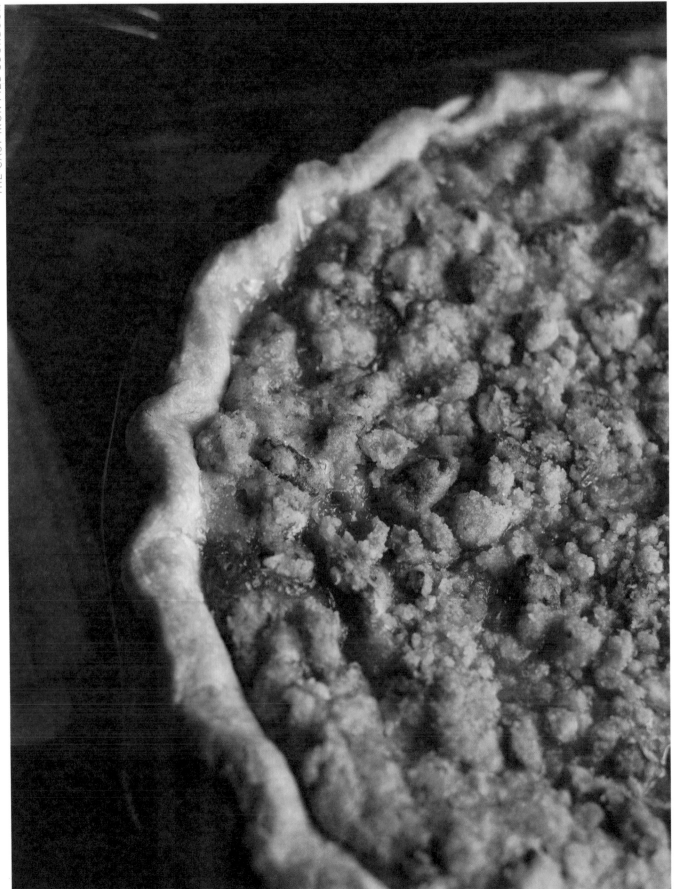

MAPLE-PEACH PECAN PIE

SERVES 8 TO 10 ✦ ACTIVE TIME: 30 MINUTES ✦ START TO FINISH: 75 MINUTES

Peaches are so delicious! Paired with pecans in this maple-kissed pie, the result is a dessert that will disappear in one sitting.

1 flaky pastry crust recipe for a single crust (see page 35)

Filling

2 cups fresh peaches, peeled, pitted, and cut into ¼-inch slices (see page 66)

3 tablespoons peach preserves

¼ cup sugar

¼ cup maple sugar

½ cup sour cream

2 egg yolks

3 tablespoons all-purpose flour

½ teaspoon vanilla extract

Topping

½ cup all-purpose flour

½ cup dark brown sugar

¼ cup 100% natural maple syrup

1 cup chopped pecan pieces

1 teaspoon ground cinnamon

¼ cup butter, melted

1. Preheat the oven to 425 degrees.

2. In a small bowl, mix the peaches and preserves and place them into the pie crust. In another bowl, mix the sugars, sour cream, egg yolks, flour, and vanilla and pour over the peaches. Put the skillet in the oven and bake for 30 minutes.

3. While the pie is baking, prepare the topping. In a bowl, mix the flour, sugar, maple syrup, pecans, cinnamon, and butter until it forms a coarse meal.

4. When the pie has cooked for 30 minutes, carefully take it out, sprinkle the crumbs on top, and replace in the oven to finish cooking, another 15 to 20 minutes, or until a knife inserted in the center comes out clean.

SALTED-CARAMEL PECAN PIE

SERVES 8 TO 10 ✦ ACTIVE TIME: 45 MINUTES ✦ START TO FINISH: 90 MINUTES

I'm a big fan of the salty-sweet confection craze, which features many kinds of salted-caramel foods. This recipe is a twist on traditional pecan pie, as the filling is cooked until it almost caramelizes. This gooey, almost smoky filling is topped with mixed-salted nuts in addition to pecans.

1 flaky pastry crust recipe for a single crust (see page 35)

½ cup pecan pieces

1½ cups mixed salted nuts

1¾ cups granulated sugar

⅓ cup dark corn syrup

¼ cup water

¾ cup heavy cream

2 tablespoons dark rum

1 teaspoon salt

3 large eggs, beaten

1. Preheat the oven to 350 degrees.

2. In a small bowl, combine the pecan pieces with the salted nuts and stir to combine. Set aside.

3. In a large, heavy-bottomed saucepan over medium heat, combine the sugar, corn syrup, and water. Cook, stirring constantly, until sugar is completely dissolved. Increase heat to medium-high and, while stirring, bring the mixture to a boil. Continue to stir as the mixture bubbles and begins to turn dark brown, about 10 minutes. Just before it starts to smoke, remove it from the heat.

4. Stand back from the saucepan and using a long-handled spoon, add the cream. The mixture will spatter. Stir until combined and settled. Return the saucepan to the heat. Add the rum and salt. Cook on medium-low until the mixture is smooth, another few minutes.

5. Ladle the mixture into a large bowl and allow to cool.

6. When cool, use a whisk and add the eggs. Pour the mixture into the pie crust. Sprinkle with the pecan/salted nut combination.

7. Put the skillet in the oven and bake for about 45 minutes or until a knife inserted toward the middle comes out clean.

8. Cool completely before serving. Serve with fresh whipped cream sprinkled with more salted nuts if desired.

CHOCOLATE-MOUSSE PECAN PIE

**SERVES 6 TO 8 ✦ ACTIVE TIME: 40 MINUTES ✦
START TO FINISH: SEVERAL HOURS OR OVERNIGHT**

Doesn't the name of this pie sound decadent? A combination of chocolate mousse and the buttery richness of pecans? Well, it is decadent in its flavor, but it is super-simple to make—it doesn't even need to be baked. Time to indulge!

**1 baked crust
(see page 32)**

½ cup coarsely chopped pecans, toasted

12 ounces semisweet chocolate morsels

2½ cups heavy cream, divided

1 tablespoon bourbon

1 teaspoon vanilla extract

1. Preheat the oven to 350 degrees.

2. Spread the pecan pieces on a cookie sheet. Bake for about 8 minutes, checking on the nuts after 5 minutes to be sure they don't burn. Remove when just starting to brown. Allow to cool.

3. Put the chocolate morsels in a microwave-safe bowl. Add ½ cup of the cream and stir. Microwave on high in 30-second increments, stirring after each. When just melted, stir in the bourbon and vanilla. Let stand for about 5 minutes.

4. In a large bowl, beat the remaining 2 cups of cream at medium-high speed with an electric mixer for about 3 minutes or until medium peaks form. Fold the chocolate mixture into the whipped cream. Pour the chocolate into the pie crust, spreading with the back of a spoon to distribute evenly. Sprinkle the toasted pecans over the top.

5. Refrigerate for several hours before serving.

GREEK-STYLE WALNUT PIE

SERVES 8 TO 10 ✦ ACTIVE TIME: 90 MINUTES ✦ START TO FINISH: SEVERAL HOURS

If you like the Greek pastry Baklava, which is a nut-rich treat with honey and lemon, you'll love this pie. It's intense, and a little goes a long way…but you'll be back for more.

1 flaky pastry crust recipe for a double crust (see page 35)

2½ cups finely chopped walnuts

¼ cup packed brown sugar

2 tablespoons granulated sugar

1½ teaspoons ground cinnamon

¾ cup butter, split into 3 (¼ cup) rations, melted, plus 1 tablespoon for greasing the skillet

¾ cup honey

1 tablespoon fresh squeezed lemon juice

1. Preheat the oven to 325 degrees.

2. In a medium bowl, mix walnuts, brown sugar, granulated sugar, and the cinnamon.

3. Put the skillet over medium heat and melt the butter in it. Carefully remove pan from heat.

4. Place 1 of the piecrusts in the skillet. Pour ¼ cup of melted butter over the bottom of the pie crust. Spread the walnut mixture evenly over butter. Melt and drizzle another ¼ cup butter over the nut mixture and place the other crust over it, crimping the edges together. Cut large slits in the middle of the top crust and drizzle the remaining ¼ cup melted butter over it, brushing to distribute evenly.

5. Put the skillet in the oven and bake for about 20 minutes. Cover the outermost edge with aluminum foil in the last 10 minutes of baking to prevent it from burning. Bake an additional 30 to 35 minutes or until golden brown.

6. When pie is nearly finished, put honey and lemon in a small saucepan. Heat over medium heat, stir, and cook, stirring constantly, until mixture is almost watery in consistency.

7. Remove pie from the oven and slowly and carefully pour the honey-lemon mixture over the top, allowing it to penetrate and drizzle into the crust.

8. Allow pie to cool for several hours before serving.

153

PEANUT BUTTER PIE

SERVES 8 TO 10 ✦ ACTIVE TIME: 30 MINUTES ✦ START TO FINISH: 90 MINUTES

Yes, peanut butter pie. And this pie tastes as amazing as it sounds. If you're looking for a peanut butter-cup kind of experience, you can also bathe the top in chocolate when cool. Try it, you'll love it.

1 chocolate graham cracker crust (see page 40)

3 eggs

1 cup dark corn syrup

½ cup sugar

½ cup creamy all-natural peanut butter (with no added sugar)

½ teaspoon vanilla extract

1 cup salted peanuts (the higher the quality, the better)

6 ounces semi-sweet chocolate morsels (if desired)

Pecans, peanuts, or walnuts as garnish (if desired)

1. Preheat the oven to 350 degrees.

2. In a large bowl, whisk the eggs until thoroughly combined. Add corn syrup and sugar, and whisk until sugar is completely dissolved. Whisk in the peanut butter and vanilla until smooth and combined. Don't over-whisk it.

3. Pour filling into the pie crust and sprinkle with the salted whole peanuts.

4. Put the skillet in the oven and bake for about 60 minutes or until a knife inserted toward the middle comes out clean. If the edge of the crust starts to overly brown, remove the skillet from the oven and put tin foil over the exposed crust until the filling is set. Allow to cool completely.

5. If you'd like to top with chocolate, put the morsels in a microwave bowl and heat in 15-second increments, stirring after each, until pieces are just melted. Drizzle over cooled pie and refrigerate until hard. Garnish with pecans, peanuts, or walnuts, if desired.

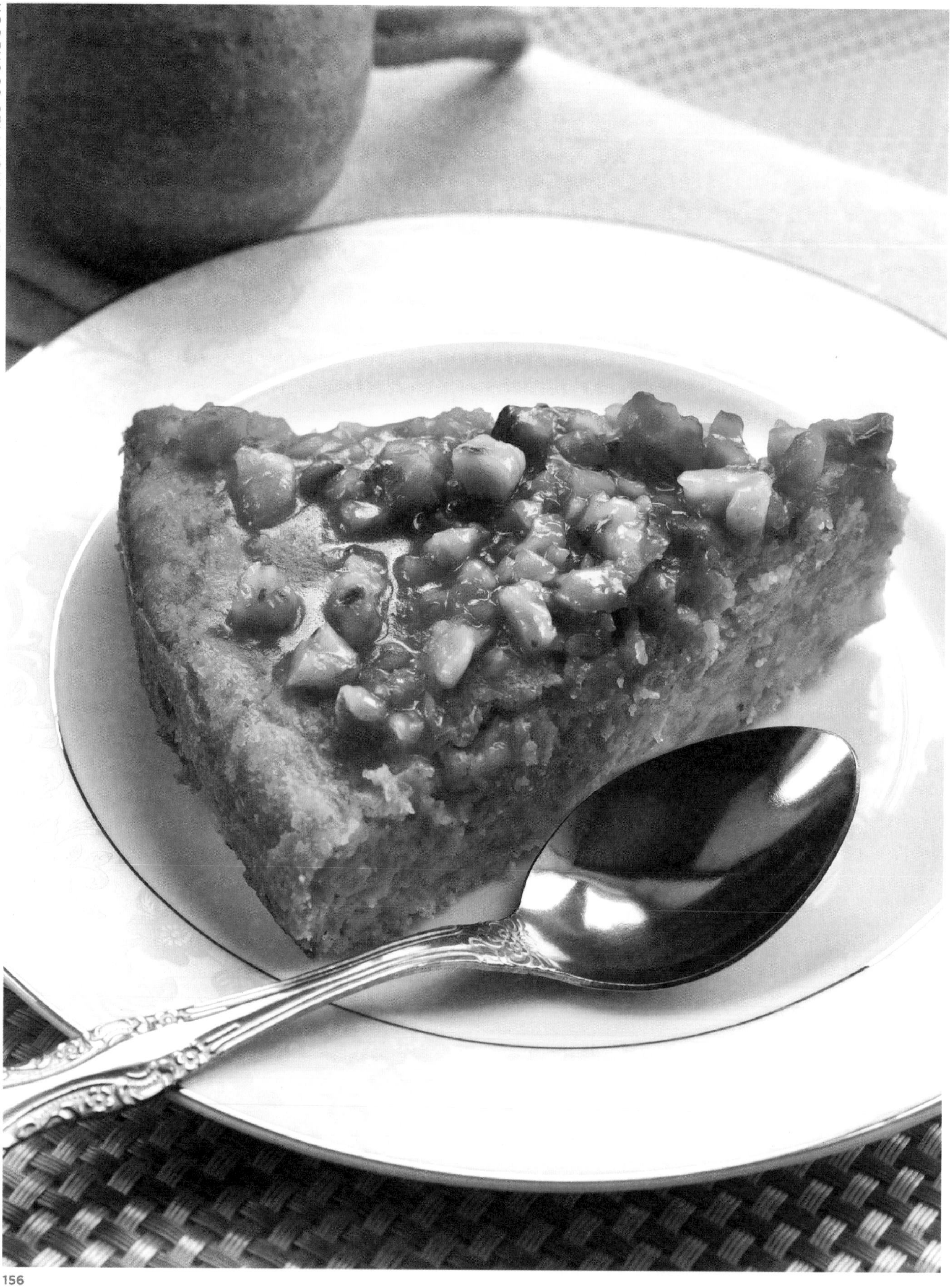

PUMPKIN-WALNUT PIE

SERVES 6 TO 8 ✦ ACTIVE TIME: 30 MINUTES ✦ START TO FINISH: 75 MINUTES

If you want to dress up a basic pumpkin pie and add a delicious nutty-buttery taste, try this recipe. The topping is so tasty!

1 flaky pastry crust recipe for a single crust (see page 35)

1 (15-oz.) can pumpkin puree (not pumpkin pie mix)

1 (14-oz.) can sweetened condensed milk (not evaporated)

2 eggs

2 tablespoons 100% natural maple syrup (preferably Grade B dark)

½ teaspoon ground cinnamon

¼ teaspoon ground ginger

¼ teaspoon ground nutmeg

¼ cup packed brown sugar

¼ cup finely chopped walnuts

2 tablespoons flour

2 tablespoons butter, chilled and cut into pieces

1. Preheat the oven to 425 degrees.

2. In a large bowl, combine the pumpkin puree, sweetened condensed milk, eggs, maple syrup, and spices. Whisk or stir until thoroughly combined. Pour into unbaked pie crust. Put the skillet in the oven and bake for 10 minutes

3. While pie is baking, in a small bowl, combine the brown sugar, walnuts, and flour. Work in the butter with your fingers until the mixture is crumbly.

4. Reduce the oven temperature to 350 degrees. Carefully take the pie out of the oven and top with the brown sugar/walnut mixture, distributing evenly. Use foil to cover the edges of the crust to prevent them from burning.

5. Return skillet to the oven and bake 30 to 35 minutes or until a knife inserted about an inch from the edge comes out clean. Allow to cool completely, and then refrigerate until ready to serve.

6. Serve with fresh whipped cream or French vanilla ice cream.

PUMPKIN-PECAN PIE

SERVES 6 TO 8 ✦ ACTIVE TIME: 30 MINUTES ✦ START TO FINISH: 75 MINUTES

This is a variation of the pumpkin-walnut pie, and its flavor is intensified by using a nut crust as a base. The result is a kind of pumpkin pie-pecan "sandwich." Yum!

1 pecan nut crust
(see page 44)

1 (15-oz.) can pumpkin
puree (not pumpkin pie
mix)

1 (14-oz.) can sweetened
condensed milk (not
evaporated)

2 eggs

2 tablespoons 100%
natural maple syrup
(preferably Grade B
dark)

½ teaspoon ground
cinnamon

¼ teaspoon ground
ginger

¼ teaspoon ground
nutmeg

¼ cup packed brown
sugar

¼ cup finely chopped
pecans

2 tablespoons flour

2 tablespoons butter,
chilled and cut into
pieces

1. Preheat the oven to 425 degrees.

2. In a large bowl, combine the pumpkin puree, sweetened condensed milk, eggs, maple syrup, and spices. Whisk or stir until thoroughly combined. Pour into unbaked pie crust. Put the skillet in the oven and bake for 10 minutes

3. While pie is baking, in a small bowl, combine the brown sugar, pecans, and flour. Work in the butter with your fingers until the mixture is crumbly.

4. Reduce the oven temperature to 350 degrees. Carefully take the pie out of the oven and top with the brown sugar/pecan mixture, distributing evenly. Use foil to cover the edges of the crust to prevent them from burning.

5. Return skillet to the oven and bake 30 to 35 minutes or until a knife inserted about an inch from the edge comes out clean. Allow to cool completely, and then refrigerate until ready to serve.

6. Serve with fresh whipped cream or French vanilla ice cream.

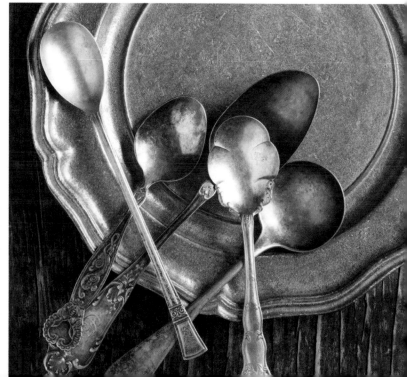

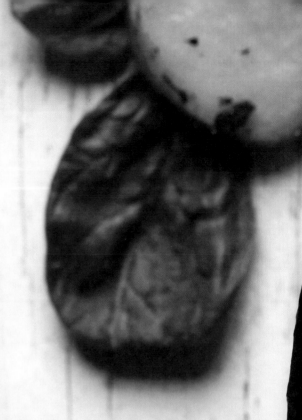

QUICHES

Quiche is a dish associated with France, and that's because the first widely popular quiche in the US was the traditional quiche "Lorraine," named after a region in France. Quiches are also found in many flavors in French patisseries (pastry shops), and so we Americans associate them with the haute cuisine of France. The region of Lorraine actually borders Germany, Luxembourg, and Belgium, and it's said that the Germans originally produced this egg-based, cheese-and-meat-filled "pie." Whatever its origins, the quiche is now a staple dish in many parts of the world, and certainly loved in the US. It's a savory pie that can be filled with nearly any combination of vegetables, meats, and cheeses—even fish. A fresh-baked quiche and a salad of leafy greens with a vinaigrette has come to define an elegant lunch, but it also makes a great dinner.

QUICHE LORRAINE

SERVES 6 TO 8 ✦ ACTIVE TIME: 30 MINUTES ✦ START TO FINISH: 60 MINUTES

There's a reason this recipe has become a household name around the world: it's fabulous! Use heavy cream for a suppleness and richness that you can't get from half-and-half. It may be more fattening, but it's also more delicious. It seems like cheese should be added to this, but the classic French quiche Lorraine does not have it. Celebrate France when you eat this and enjoy with a glass of wine. Voilà!

1 baked crust
(see page 32)

½-¾ pound thick-cut
bacon, cut into ¼-inch
pieces

3 large eggs

2 cups heavy cream

¾ teaspoon coarse salt

¼ teaspoon freshly
ground pepper

1. Preheat the oven to 400 degrees.

2. In a skillet, sauté the bacon pieces until just crispy, about 10 minutes. Use a slotted spoon to gather the pieces and put them on a plate lined with a paper towel to absorb the grease.

3. In a large bowl, whisk the eggs and cream until thoroughly combined. Add the salt and pepper and stir.

4. Pour the egg mixture into the crust-lined cast-iron skillet and sprinkle with the bacon pieces.

5. Put the skillet in the oven and bake for about 30 minutes or until the quiche is puffy and golden brown and the eggs are set.

6. Allow to sit for 10 minutes before slicing and serving.

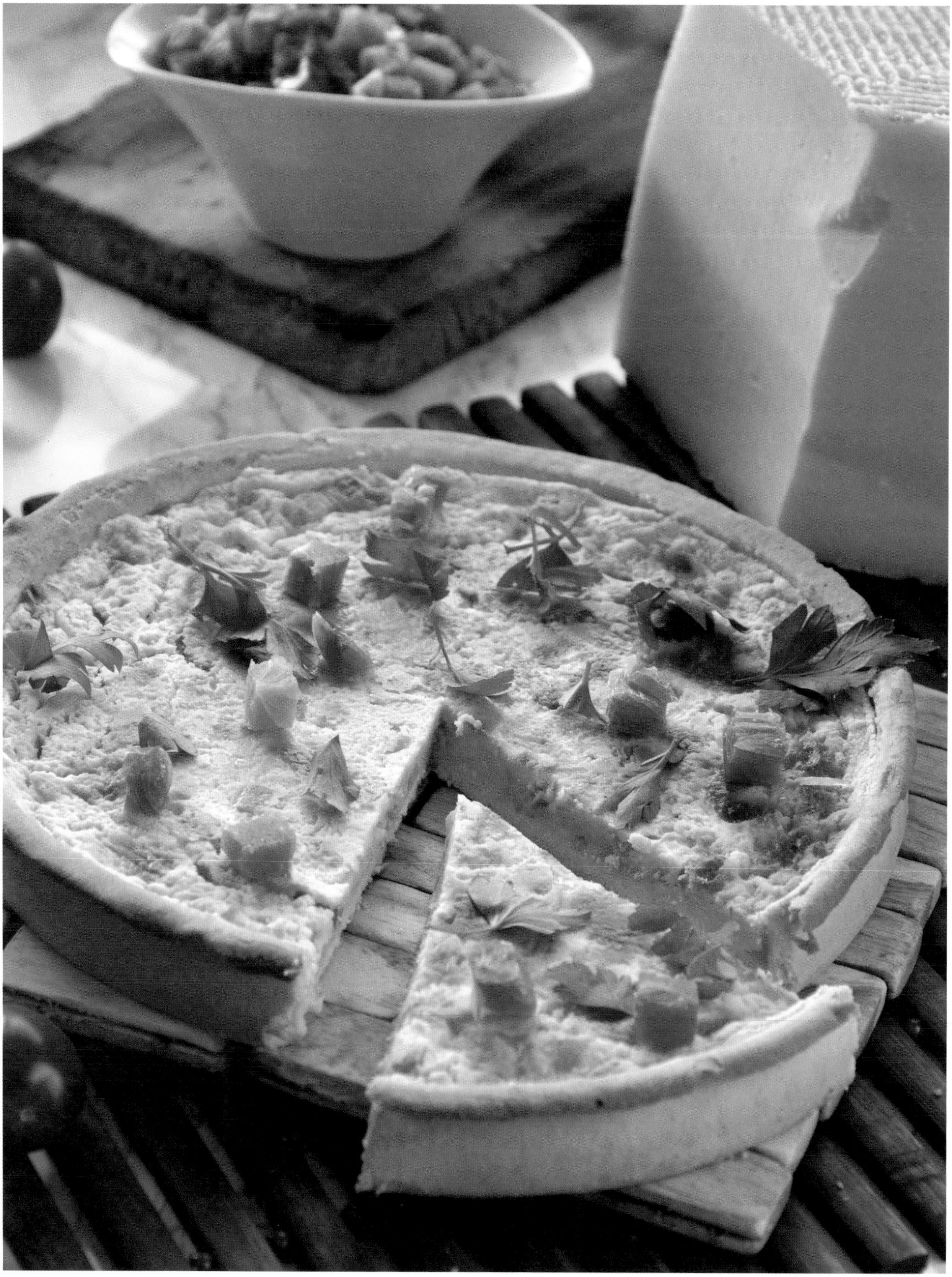

HAM AND CHEDDAR QUICHE

SERVES 6 TO 8 ✦ ACTIVE TIME: 40 MINUTES ✦ START TO FINISH: 90 MINUTES

What a combo! This quiche is rich with the salty goodness of fresh ham and the gooey deliciousness of cheddar cheese. The higher quality the ingredients you select, the more flavorful it is, so don't skimp on this one.

1 baked crust
(see page 32)

2 tablespoons brown mustard

1 cup diced fully cooked ham

1 cup shredded sharp cheddar cheese

4 eggs

1½ cups whole milk or half-and-half

1 teaspoon salt

1 teaspoon ground pepper

Paprika (optional)

1. Preheat the oven to 350 degrees.

2. With the crust in the skillet, use a pastry brush or the back of a spoon to spread the mustard on the bottom and sides.

3. Sprinkle the ham pieces and shredded cheddar evenly over the bottom of the pie.

4. In a medium bowl, whisk the eggs until thoroughly combined. Add the milk, salt, and pepper and whisk to combine.

5. Pour the egg mixture over the meat and cheese, shaking the pan gently to distribute evenly and settle the liquid. If desired, sprinkle the top with paprika.

6. Put the skillet in the oven and bake for 35 to 40 minutes or until the quiche is puffy and golden brown and the eggs are set.

7. Allow to sit for 10 minutes before slicing and serving.

BACON AND ZUCCHINI QUICHE

SERVES 6 TO 8 ✦ ACTIVE TIME: 45 MINUTES ✦ START TO FINISH: 90 MINUTES

Crisp, salty bacon is the perfect complement to zucchini in this late-summer quiche. I like to add a garlic-herb chèvre to further highlight these ingredients.

1 baked crust
(see page 32)

½-¾ pound thick-cut
bacon, cut into pieces

1 small zucchini,
cut into thin rounds

1 clove garlic, minced

4 eggs

1½ cups half-and-half

½ teaspoon salt

½ teaspoon freshly
ground pepper

3-5 ounces garlic-herb
chèvre

1. Preheat the oven to 350 degrees.

2. In a skillet, sauté the bacon pieces until just crispy, about 10 minutes. Use a slotted spoon to gather the pieces and put them on a plate lined with a paper towel to absorb the grease.

3. Add the zucchini pieces and garlic to the bacon fat, reduce the heat, and stir. Cook until zucchini is just soft, about 10 minutes.

4. Sprinkle the bacon pieces on the bottom of the pie crust, and use a slotted spoon to put the zucchini over it. Dot the mixture with the garlic-herb chèvre.

5. In a medium bowl, whisk the eggs until thoroughly combined. Add the half-and-half and salt and pepper, and whisk to combine.

6. Pour the egg mixture over the other ingredients, shaking the pan gently to distribute evenly.

7. Put the skillet in the oven and bake for 35 to 40 minutes or until the quiche is puffy and golden brown and the eggs are set. Use pot holders or oven mitts to take the skillet out of the oven.

8. Allow to sit for 10 minutes before slicing and serving.

TEX MEX QUICHE

SERVES 6 TO 8 ✦ ACTIVE TIME: 60 MINUTES ✦ START TO FINISH: 2 HOURS

What characterizes a food as Tex-Mex? For me it's the combination of smoky, hot flavors with fresh, bright flavors, representing the heat and intensity of South of the Border.

For the crust

1 (9-oz.) bag yellow corn tortilla chips

7 tablespoons butter

½ teaspoon cayenne pepper

For the filling

2 tablespoons olive oil

½ pound sausage

2 cloves garlic, minced

¼ cup minced yellow onion

½ cup green pepper, seeded, cored, and cut into dime-sized pieces

¼ cup red pepper, seeded, cored, and cut into dime-sized pieces

1 small jalapeño pepper, seeded and cut into small pieces

¾ cup shredded Monterey Jack cheese

5 large eggs

1½ cups half-and-half

1 tablespoon salt

1 tablespoon freshly ground black pepper

1. Preheat the oven to 350 degrees.

2. Put the chips in a food processor and pulse until they form crumbs, or put in a large plastic bag and crush with a rolling pin or meat tenderizer.

3. Put 2 cups of the crushed chips in a large bowl. Add 5 tablespoons melted butter and the cayenne pepper. Stir to combine.

4. Grease the cast-iron skillet liberally with the additional 2 tablespoons of butter.

5. Press the tortilla chip mixture lightly into skillet to form a crust. Bake until just golden, about 10 minutes. Remove from oven, and allow crust to cool.

1. Preheat the oven to 350 degrees.

2. In a skillet, heat the olive oil over medium heat and add the sausage meat. Cook, stirring, to break up the meat into crumbles. When it is no longer pink throughout, transfer the meat with a slotted spoon onto a plate lined with a paper towel to soak up the grease.

3. Add the onion and garlic to the pan and stir, cooking for about 3 minutes. Add the peppers and, if the pan seems dry, another tablespoon of olive oil. Cook the vegetables for about 6 minutes, until just softening, and add back the sausage meat. Stir to combine and remove from the heat.

4. Sprinkle about half the shredded cheese over the taco shell crust, and top with the sausage/pepper/onion mixture. Spread evenly. Sprinkle the remaining cheese on top.

5. In a large bowl, whisk the eggs until thoroughly combined. Add the half-and-half, salt, and pepper, and whisk to combine. Pour the egg mixture over the other ingredients, shaking the pan gently to distribute evenly.

6. Put the skillet in the oven and bake for 30 to 40 minutes or until the quiche is puffy and golden brown and the eggs are set. A knife inserted in the center should come out clean.

7. Allow to sit for about 30 minutes before slicing and serving.

BEET AND CHÈVRE QUICHE

SERVES 6 TO 8 ✦ ACTIVE TIME: 45 MINUTES ✦ START TO FINISH: 2 HOURS

I love beets. They're beautiful and they're good for you. And they taste great. All good reasons to cook them up and put them in a quiche, where their color, texture, and flavor all work beautifully. Add fresh goat cheese (chèvre) and a hint of thyme, and you have an elegant, easy, and fabulous meal.

1 flaky pastry crust recipe for a single crust (see page 35)

4 or 5 red or golden beets (or a combination), peeled and sliced thin

2 tablespoons yellow onions, minced

1 teaspoon olive oil

6 eggs

1½ cups whole milk

2 teaspoons dried thyme

2 cloves garlic, pressed

4 ounces fresh goat cheese (chèvre)

1. Preheat the oven to 400 degrees.

2. Put the beet slices and minced onion in a pouch of heavy duty aluminum foil. Drizzle with olive oil and close up securely. Put the pouch in the oven and roast the beets and onions for about 20 minutes until soft, checking after 10 to 15 minutes. Remove pouch from oven and let sit while you prep the other ingredients.

3. In a large bowl, whisk the eggs until thoroughly combined. Add the milk, thyme, and garlic, and whisk to combine.

4. Carefully open the pouch of beets and onions and distribute over the pie crust. Pour the egg mixture over this, and dot with pieces of the goat cheese.

5. Cover the skillet with foil and bake for 40 minutes. Remove foil from skillet and continue to bake another 10 to 15 minutes or until the quiche is golden brown and the eggs are set. A knife inserted in the center should come out clean.

6. Allow to sit for about 30 minutes before slicing and serving.

SAUSAGE AND FETA QUICHE

SERVES 6 TO 8 ✦ ACTIVE TIME: 45 MINUTES ✦ START TO FINISH: 90 MINUTES

This is a really yummy combination, made all the better by adding some Kalamata olives. If you can't get to Greece, make this quiche and find a sunny spot. You'll be transported.

1 baked crust
(see page 32)

2 tablespoons olive oil

½ pound Italian sausage

¼ cup diced red onion

1 small tomato, seeds removed, diced

¼ cup Kalamata olives, halved

½ cup crumbled feta cheese

4 eggs

2 cups whole milk

1 teaspoon salt

1 teaspoon fresh ground pepper

1. Preheat the oven to 350 degrees.

2. In a skillet, heat the olive oil over medium heat and add the sausage meat. Cook, stirring, to break up the meat into crumbles. When it is no longer pink throughout, transfer the meat with a slotted spoon onto a plate lined with a paper towel to soak up the grease.

3. Add the onion to the skillet and stir, cooking for about 3 minutes. Add the sausage back to the pan, and add the tomato and olives. Stir to combine and remove from the heat. Allow to cool slightly.

4. In a large bowl, whisk the eggs until thoroughly combined. Add the milk, salt, and pepper, and whisk to combine. Fill the pie crust with the meat and vegetables. Sprinkle the crumbled feta evenly over the mixture. Pour the egg mixture over the other ingredients, shaking the pan gently to distribute evenly.

5. Put the skillet in the oven and bake for 30 to 40 minutes or until the quiche is puffy and golden brown and the eggs are set. A knife inserted in the center should come out clean.

6. Allow to sit for about 20 minutes before slicing and serving.

CARAMELIZED ONION, PANCETTA, AND SUMMER SQUASH QUICHE

SERVES 6 TO 8 ✦ ACTIVE TIME: 45 MINUTES ✦ START TO FINISH: 90 MINUTES

Summer squash is either yellow squash or zucchini. It's best to use a combination. With the onions and pancetta, the result is a complete meal in a pan. Simple and satisfying.

1 baked crust
(see page 32)

1 tablespoon olive oil

1 tablespoon butter

4 yellow onions,
sliced thin

¼ to ½ pound pancetta
(or bacon), cut into
pieces

¾ cup yellow squash,
sliced very thin

½ cup zucchini,
sliced thin

4 eggs

1½ cups half-and-half

½ teaspoon salt

¼ teaspoon pepper

Parmesan cheese,
if desired

1. In a large skillet, melt the olive oil and butter together. Add the onions and, working over a low flame, cook and stir the onions as they soften and brown. Be careful not to let them burn. After about 5 minutes, reduce the heat and cover the skillet to further soften them, letting them cook, covered, for another 3 to 4 minutes. Add the squash and continue to cook until it is wilted, about 3 minutes. Add the pancetta pieces, stir to combine, and remove from heat. Drain any liquid from the pan.

2. In a large bowl, whisk the eggs until thoroughly combined. Add the half-and-half, salt, and pepper, and whisk to combine. Stir the onion/vegetable mix into the egg mix, and pour everything into the pie crust, shaking the pan gently to distribute evenly. Sprinkle with Parmesan cheese if desired.

3. Put the skillet in the oven and bake for 30 to 40 minutes or until the quiche is puffy and golden brown and the eggs are set. A knife inserted in the center should come out clean.

4. Allow to sit for about 20 minutes before slicing and serving.

CRAB QUICHE

SERVES 6 TO 8 ✦ ACTIVE TIME: 40 MINUTES ✦ START TO FINISH: 90 MINUTES

This recipe harkens back to the cuisine of my parents—decadent ingredients in cream and vermouth. It's easy to see why it was so popular once you taste this. It's a great Sunday brunch recipe to serve along with a big green salad and a bottle of French rosé!

1 flaky pastry crust recipe for a single crust (see page 35)

3 tablespoons unsalted butter

2 tablespoon scallions, tender parts only, thinly sliced

4 eggs

2 cups half-and-half

2 tablespoons dry Vermouth

½ teaspoon salt

¼ teaspoon cayenne pepper

1 pound lump crab meat, thawed and drained if frozen

1. Preheat the oven to 350 degrees.

2. In a skillet over medium heat, melt butter and add scallions. Cook for about 5 minutes until onions are tender.

3. In a large bowl, whisk eggs until thoroughly combined. Add the half-and-half, Vermouth, salt, and cayenne pepper, and whisk to combine. Stir the cooked onion mixture and the crabmeat into the egg mix, and pour everything into the pie crust, shaking the pan gently to distribute evenly.

4. Put the skillet in the oven and bake for about 40 minutes or until the quiche is golden brown and the eggs are set. A knife inserted in the center should come out clean.

5. Allow to sit for about 20 minutes before slicing and serving.

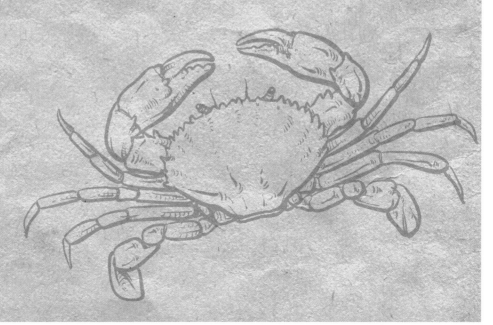

SMOKED SALMON AND DILL QUICHE

SERVES 6 TO 8 ✦ ACTIVE TIME: 30 MINUTES ✦ START TO FINISH: 90 MINUTES

Any good deli in New York City will serve smoked salmon for breakfast— typically on a bagel with a schmear of cream cheese, a few capers, and a sprig of dill. What a treat! Putting smoked salmon and dill in a quiche makes for a breakfast dish that is still fantastic for fans of the fish, but is mellower and therefore more palatable for those who might not be…though no one can resist.

1 flaky pastry crust recipe for a single crust (see page 35)

1 teaspoon Dijon mustard

1 pound smoked salmon, cut or torn into nickel-sized pieces

4 eggs

1 cup half-and-half

1 teaspoon salt

½ teaspoon ground black pepper

1 tablespoon dill, finely minced

1 (3-oz.) package cream cheese, cut into small cubes

1. Preheat the oven to 350 degrees.

2. Working with the crust in the skillet, brush the mustard over the bottom of the dough. Place the salmon pieces in the pie.

3. In a large bowl, whisk the eggs until thoroughly combined. Add the half-and-half, salt, and pepper, and whisk to combine. Add the dill and mix well.

4. Pour the egg mixture over the salmon pieces, shaking the pan gently to distribute evenly. Sprinkle the cubes of cream cheese evenly on top.

5. Put the skillet in the oven and bake for 35 to 40 minutes or until the quiche is puffy and golden brown and the eggs are set.

6. Allow to sit for 10 minutes before slicing and serving.

SPINACH AND SUN-DRIED TOMATO QUICHE

SERVES 6 TO 8 ✦ ACTIVE TIME: 40 MINUTES ✦ START TO FINISH: 90 MINUTES

If you want to impress your coworkers, make this the night before and bring it to the office for lunch. Your office mates will be drooling when they get a look at this beautiful and healthy quiche.

1 flaky crust for single crust (see page 35)

1 tablespoon butter

1 small leek, white part only, sliced thin

3 cups fresh spinach leaves, stems removed, or 1 cup frozen spinach, thawed and squeezed dry

⅔ cup chopped, drained, sun-dried tomatoes

1 (3-oz.) piece of fresh goat cheese

5 eggs

1½ cups whole milk or half-and-half

½ teaspoon salt

¼ teaspoon pepper

1 teaspoon dried thyme

½ teaspoon cayenne (if desired)

1. Preheat oven to 350 degrees.

2. In a separate small skillet over medium heat, melt butter and cook leeks, stirring, until softened, about 5 minutes.

3. Working with the crust in the skillet, scatter the spinach leaves evenly over the bottom, then sprinkle the sun-dried tomato pieces over them. Next, separate the rings of the leeks and sprinkle the pieces over the spinach and tomatoes.

4. Use a fork to crumble the goat cheese and dot the top of the pie with the cheese pieces.

5. In a medium bowl, whisk the eggs until thoroughly combined. Add the milk or half-and-half, then the salt, pepper, thyme, and cayenne of desired, and whisk to combine.

6. Pour the egg mixture over the vegetables, shaking the pan gently to distribute evenly.

7. Put the skillet in the oven and bake for 35 to 40 minutes or until the quiche is puffy and golden brown and the eggs are set.

8. Allow to sit for 10 minutes before slicing and serving.

VERY VEGGIE QUICHE

SERVES 6 TO 8 ❖ **ACTIVE TIME: 45 MINUTES** ❖ **START TO FINISH: 90 MINUTES**

This is essentially a salad in a shell—layered with color and flavor and loaded with goodness. It's easy to vary the ingredients, too, depending on what's in season.

1 savory cornmeal crust (see page 39)

4 tablespoons olive oil

1 small onion, diced

2 cloves garlic, peeled and thinly sliced

1 cup sliced mushrooms (style of your choice)

1 cup thinly sliced zucchini, rounds cut in half

1 bunch Swiss Chard, washed and chopped (stems chopped fine)

1 small carrot, peeled and sliced thin

½ to 1 cup fresh corn kernels

4 eggs

2 cups whole milk or half-and-half

1 teaspoon salt

½ teaspoon ground pepper

½ cup fresh basil leaves, chopped

1. Preheat the oven to 350 degrees.

2. In a deep sauté pan or skillet, heat the olive oil over medium heat. Add the onion and garlic and cook, stirring, until just soft, about 3 minutes. Add the mushroom and zucchini pieces and stir, cooking, for another 3 minutes. Add the Swiss chard and carrots. Stir all the vegetables together. Reduce the heat to low and put a lid on the pan. Cook, covered, for about 10 minutes, stirring occasionally to prevent sticking or burning. Stir in the corn kernels and cook another 5 minutes until all vegetables are crisp-soft. Drain any excess liquid. Remove the lid and allow to cool to room temperature.

3. In a medium bowl, whisk the eggs until thoroughly combined. Add the milk or half-and-half and salt and pepper, and whisk to combine.

4. Spread the vegetable mixture loosely over the bottom of the cornmeal crust and pour the egg mixture over it, shaking the pan gently to distribute evenly. Top with the chopped basil.

5. Put the skillet in the oven and bake for 35 to 40 minutes or until the quiche is puffy and golden brown and the eggs are set.

6. Allow to sit for 10 minutes before slicing and serving.

BROCCOLI-CHEDDAR QUICHE

SERVES 6 TO 8 ✦ ACTIVE TIME: 45 MINUTES ✦ START TO FINISH: 90 MINUTES

This is a recipe that features broccoli paired with cheddar. It's delicious heated or at room temperature, and, served with a salad, makes a great meal.

1 flaky pastry crust recipe for a single crust (see page 35)

1 teaspoon Dijon mustard

1¼ cup grated/shredded cheddar cheese

3 cups broccoli florets and stems

6 eggs

1 cup half-and-half

1 teaspoon salt

½ teaspoon ground black pepper

½ cup grated parmesan cheese

1. Preheat the oven to 350 degrees.

2. In a saucepan, steam the broccoli pieces until cooked but still crisp, about 15 minutes. Drain and rinse with cold water and set aside to dry.

3. Working with the crust in the skillet, brush the mustard over the bottom of the dough. Next, use about ¼ cup of the cheese and sprinkle it over the dough. Place the broccoli pieces in the pie.

4. In a large bowl, whisk the eggs until thoroughly combined. Add the half-and-half, salt, and pepper, and whisk to combine. Add the remaining cheese and mix well.

5. Pour the egg mixture over the broccoli pieces, shaking the pan gently to distribute evenly. Sprinkle the Parmesan over everything.

6. Put the skillet in the oven and bake for 35 to 40 minutes or until the quiche is puffy and golden brown and the eggs are set.

7. Allow to sit for 10 minutes before slicing and serving.

QUICHE WITH SAUTÉED LEEKS

SERVES 6 TO 8 ✦ ACTIVE TIME: 30 MINUTES ✦ START TO FINISH: 90 MINUTES

The leeks in this recipe are sautéed until soft and golden, which brings out their delectable mild onion flavor. Swiss or gruyere cheese is the perfect complement. This is an easy-to-make quiche that is nonetheless quite elegant. It goes great with a green salad.

1 flaky pastry crust recipe for a single crust (see page 35)

3 large leeks, white and light green parts only

2 tablespoons olive oil

4 eggs

1 cup whole milk or half-and-half

½ to ¾ cup shredded Swiss or gruyere cheese

Salt and pepper to taste

1. Preheat the oven to 400 degrees.

2. Prepare the leeks by cutting the white and light green parts only into thin slices. Separate the rings in a colander, and rinse thoroughly to remove any sand or grit. Pat dry.

3. In a skillet, heat the olive oil over medium-high heat. Add the leeks and cook, stirring, for a 1 or 2 minutes. Lower the heat and continue to cook so that the leeks become tender and golden, not overly browned, about 10 to 15 minutes. Stir frequently.

4. In a large bowl, whisk the eggs until thoroughly combined. Add the half-and-half, and whisk to combine. Add the shredded cheese and mix well. Season with salt and pepper.

5. Spread the sautéed leeks over the crust in the cast-iron skillet. Pour the egg/cheese mixture over the leeks, shaking the pan gently to distribute evenly.

6. Put the skillet in the oven and bake for about 40 minutes or until the quiche is puffy and golden brown and the eggs are set.

7. Allow to sit for 10 minutes before slicing and serving.

MUSHROOM AND SWISS CHEESE QUICHE

SERVES 6 TO 8 ✦ ACTIVE TIME: 30 MINUTES ✦ START TO FINISH: 90 MINUTES

If you want a delicious, earthy quiche that will hit the spot on a cool autumn day, then this is it. Swiss cheese is the perfect complement for mushrooms, and the cornmeal crust is a great choice for this, as it adds some texture. You can use a flaky pastry crust, too.

1 cornmeal crust
(see page 39)

4 tablespoons butter

½ pound mushrooms,
sliced thin (a mixture
of Portobello, shitake,
and white mushrooms
is ideal)

1 small leek, white part
only, sliced thin

4 eggs

2 cups whole milk

1 teaspoon salt

½ teaspoon pepper

⅛ teaspoon nutmeg

1 cup shredded Swiss
cheese

1. Preheat the oven to 350 degrees.

2. In a skillet over medium heat, melt the butter and add the mushrooms and leeks. Cook, stirring, until vegetables are soft, about 5 minutes.

3. In a large bowl, whisk eggs until thoroughly combined. Add milk, salt, pepper, and nutmeg, and whisk to combine.

4. Sprinkle half of the Swiss cheese on the pie crust. Distribute the mushroom/leek mixture over the cheese. Pour the egg mixture over everything and shake the skillet gently to evenly distribute the liquid. Sprinkle the remaining Swiss cheese on top.

5. Put the skillet in the oven and bake for 30 to 40 minutes or until the quiche is puffy and golden brown and the eggs are set.

6. Allow to sit for about 20 minutes before slicing and serving.

SWISS CHARD AND CHERRY TOMATO QUICHE

SERVES 6 TO 8 ✦ ACTIVE TIME: 45 MINUTES ✦ START TO FINISH: 90 MINUTES

These ingredients are abundant at farmer's markets in the summer, and make for a yummy and healthy quiche combo.

1 flaky pastry crust recipe for a single crust (page 35)

4 tablespoons olive oil

2 cloves garlic, peeled and thinly sliced

1 bunch Swiss Chard, washed and chopped (stems chopped fine)

10-12 cherry tomatoes, cut in half

4 eggs

2 cups whole milk or half-and-half

1 teaspoon salt

½ teaspoon ground pepper

1 teaspoon hot sauce, if desired

1. Preheat the oven to 350 degrees.

2. In a skillet, heat the olive oil over medium heat. Add the garlic and Swiss Chard and cook, stirring, until Chard is soft, about 8 to 10 minutes. Add the cherry tomato halves and continue to cook for a couple of minutes. Drain excess liquid from pan.

3. In a large bowl, whisk the eggs until thoroughly combined. Add the milk or half-and-half and salt and pepper, and whisk to combine. Add the chard and tomato mixture, and the hot sauce, if desired. Pour the egg mixture over everything and shake the skillet gently to evenly distribute the liquid.

4. Put the skillet in the oven and bake for 35 to 40 minutes or until the quiche is puffy and golden brown and the eggs are set.

5. Allow to sit for 10 minutes before slicing and serving.

SWEET TARTS & GALETTES

This chapter should be called The Fastest Way to a Great Dessert. Tarts are essentially pared-down pies that need only a single crust and hold less filling. Galettes are basically fruit (or the filling of your choice, as there are savory galettes as well, see the next chapter) piled up on top of a crust that's crimped around the edges to hold in the filling. They are so easy to make and showcase their bright fruit fillings so perfectly. Once you get the hang of these simple yet sensational desserts, you'll want to play with the filling ingredients. Consider adding spices like cinnamon, ginger or nutmeg. Vary the jams you use as a fruit-enhancing base on the crusts, playing with different flavors. You can also add some liqueur to the jam or even the fruit filling. The galettes, in particular, beg to be topped with ice cream or whipped cream. Go for it!

FRENCH APPLE TART

**SERVES 6 TO 8 ✦ ACTIVE TIME: 60 MINUTES ✦
START TO FINISH: SEVERAL HOURS OR OVERNIGHT**

*Cast-iron skillets caramelize fruits to perfection. This recipe is the quintessential example.
It's what the French call "tarte tatin," and for them it's a national treasure.*

1 cup flour

½ teaspoon salt

1 tablespoon sugar

6 tablespoons unsalted
butter, cut into small
pieces

3 tablespoons ice water

1 cup (2 sticks) unsalted
butter, cut into small
pieces

1½ cups sugar

8 to 10 apples, peeled,
cored, and halved

1. To make the pastry, whisk together the flour, salt, and sugar in a large bowl.
Using your fingers, work the butter into the flour mixture until you have
coarse clumps. Sprinkle the ice water over the mixture and continue to work
it with your hands until it just holds together. Shape it into a ball, wrap it in
plastic wrap, and refrigerate it for at least one hour, but even overnight.

2. Preparation for the tart starts in the skillet. Place the pieces of butter evenly
over the bottom of the skillet, then sprinkle the sugar evenly over everything.
Next, start placing the apple halves in a circular pattern, starting on the outside
of the pan and working in. The halves should support each other and all face
the same direction. Place either 1 or 2 halves in the center when finished
working around the outside. As the cake bakes, the slices will slide down a bit.

3. Place the skillet on the oven and turn the heat to medium-high. Cook the
apples in the pan, uncovered, until the sugar and butter start to caramelize,
about 35 minutes. While they're cooking, spoon some of the melted juices over
the apples (but don't overdo it).

4. Preheat the oven to 400 degrees, and position a rack in the center.

5. Take the chilled dough out of the refrigerator and working on a lightly
floured surface, roll it out into a circle just big enough to cover the skillet
(about 12 to 14 inches). Gently drape the pastry over the apples, tucking
the pastry in around the sides.

6. Put the skillet in the oven and bake for about 25 minutes, until the pastry is
golden brown.

7. Remove the skillet from the oven and allow to cool for about 5 minutes.
Find a plate that is an inch or two larger than the top of the skillet and place
it over the top. You will be inverting the tart onto the plate. Be sure to use oven
mitts or secure pot holders, as the skillet will be hot.

8. Holding the plate tightly against the top of the skillet, turn the skillet over so
the plate is now on the bottom. If some of the apples are stuck to the bottom,
gently remove them and place them on the tart.

9. Allow to cool a few more minutes, or set aside until ready to serve (it's better if
it's served warm).

GLUTEN-FREE RASPBERRY ALMOND TART

SERVES 6 TO 8 ✦ ACTIVE TIME: 30 MINUTES ✦ START TO FINISH: 90 MINUTES

What's amazing about this dessert is the sweetness of the raspberries with the nutty hints of almond. They are a great pair. And of course the custard is creamy, the colors are gorgeous, and the overall effect is of something irresistible.

1 gluten-free crust (see page 36)

5 tablespoons unsalted butter, softened

½ cup sugar, plus 1 tablespoon

Dash of salt

1 egg, plus 1 egg white

¾ cup almond flour

½ teaspoon almond extract

1½ cups fresh raspberries

1. Preheat the oven to 375 degrees.

2. In a large bowl, cream butter with sugar until mixture is light and fluffy. Add salt.

3. Stir in the egg and egg white until thoroughly combined, then the flour and almond extract. In a separate bowl, stir the raspberries with the extra tablespoon of sugar.

4. Sprinkle about ⅓ of the berries on the crust. Top with the almond/egg mixture, and add the remaining raspberries on top.

5. Put the skillet in the oven and bake for about 40 to 45 minutes, until a knife inserted near the center comes out clean.

6. Allow to cool completely.

GINGER KEY LIME TART

SERVES 6 TO 8 ✦ ACTIVE TIME: 40 MINUTES ✦ START TO FINISH: 60 MINUTES

To complement the zestiness of the key lime, the tart is baked in a gingersnap crust spiked with fresh ginger, which itself has a bright, zingy flavor. The result is an explosion in your mouth.

8-10 gingersnap cookies

1 teaspoon fresh grated ginger

½ cup (8 tablespoons) unsalted butter, divided into portions of 6 tablespoons and 2 tablespoons

1 (14-oz.) can sweetened condensed milk

½ cup key lime juice

4 large egg yolks

1 tablespoon vanilla extract

1. Preheat the oven to 350 degrees.

2. In a food processor, grind the cookie pieces until they form crumbs. If you don't have a food processor, you can also put the cookie halves in a resealable plastic bag and use a rolling pin to grind them into crumbs.

3. Put the crumbs in a bowl and add the ginger. Stir in the 6 tablespoons of melted butter. Heat the remaining 2 tablespoons until just melted and put the butter in the cast-iron skillet to coat the bottom. Press the cookie crumb mixture into the skillet, extending the crust about half way up the sides of the skillet.

4. Bake until the crust is firm, about 10 minutes. Allow to cool. Reduce oven temperature to 325.

5. In a medium bowl, combine the condensed milk, key lime juice, egg yolks, and vanilla. Pour the filling into the crust.

6. Put the skillet in the oven and bake for about 20 to 30 minutes, until the liquid has set into a soft custard.

7. Allow to cool completely before serving.

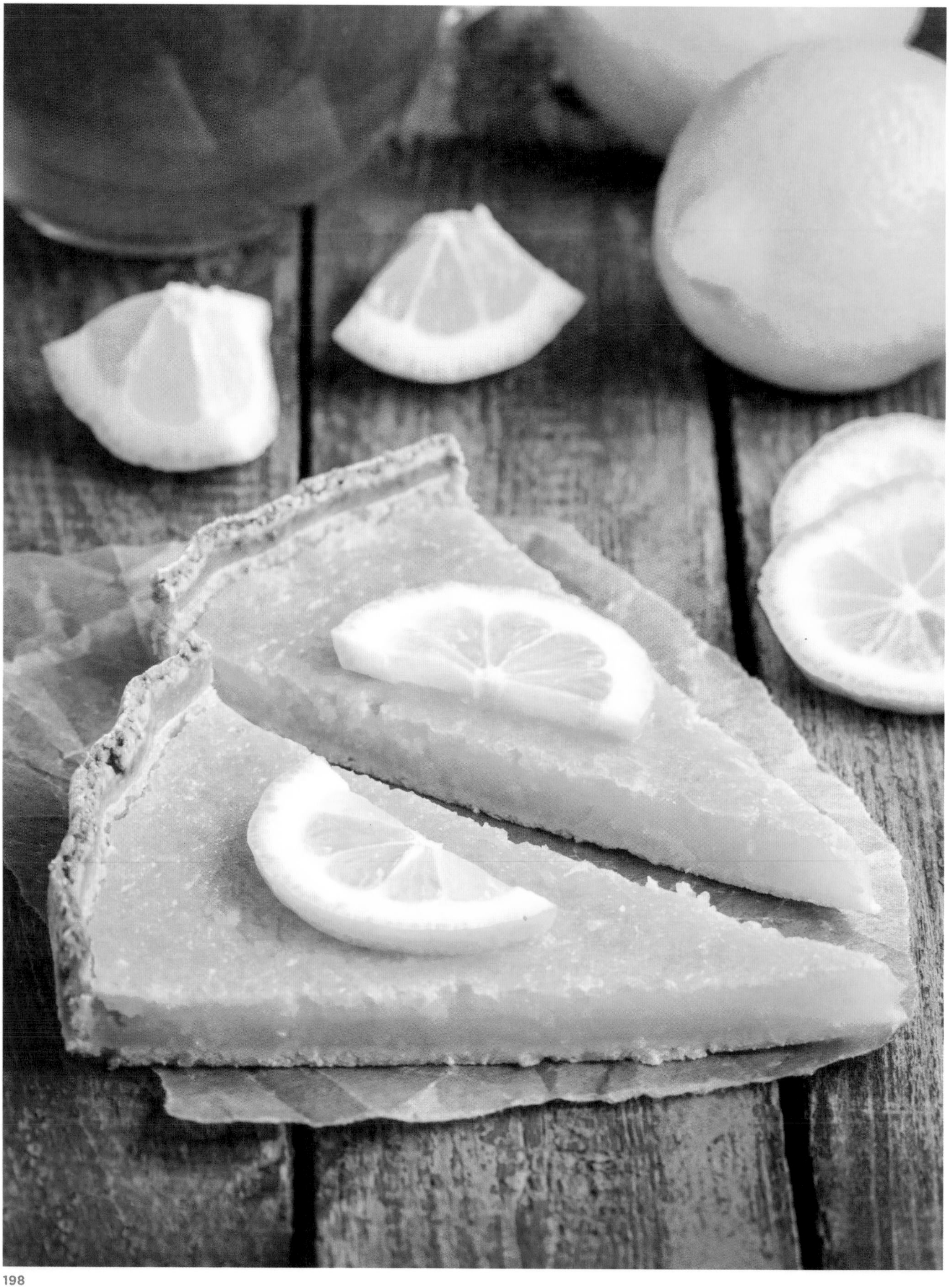

DOUBLE LEMON TART

SERVES 6 TO 8 ♦ ACTIVE TIME: 30 MINUTES ♦ START TO FINISH: 60 MINUTES

Lemons are like sunshine—they brighten everything! Very thinly sliced lemons sit atop a lemon-drenched custard nestled in a graham cracker crust and make a dessert whose flavor shines through from the first to last bites.

1 graham cracker crust (see page 40)

1 (14-oz.) can sweetened condensed milk

½ cup fresh squeezed lemon juice

4 large egg yolks

1 tablespoon vanilla extract

1 lemon, very thinly sliced, seeds removed

1. Preheat the oven to 325 degrees.

2. In a medium bowl, combine the condensed milk, lemon juice, egg yolks, and vanilla. Pour the filling into the crust. Top with the very thin slices of lemon, arranged in a decorative pattern.

3. Put the skillet in the oven and bake for about 20 minutes, until the liquid has set into a soft custard.

4. Allow to cool completely before serving.

STRAWBERRY-KIWI TART

SERVES 6 TO 8 ✦ ACTIVE TIME: 90 MINUTES ✦ START TO FINISH: SEVERAL HOURS

This is one of those desserts you marvel at in the display case of a high-end grocery store. It always looks perfect. When you make one yourself, you'll find that it's quite simple, and looks just as impressive.

1 baked crust
(see page 35)

½ cup (4 ounces)
cream cheese, at room
temperature

½ cup sugar

1 teaspoon vanilla
extract

1 cup heavy cream

1½ cups fresh
strawberries, stems
removed and sliced
in half

3 medium kiwis, peeled
and sliced widthwise

3 tablespoons seedless
strawberry jam

1 tablespoon water

1. In a large bowl, cream the softened cream cheese with the sugar, stirring until very smooth. Add the vanilla.

2. In a separate bowl, whip the cream with an electric mixer on high until it forms stiff peaks. Fold the cream into the cheese mixture until it's fully incorporated. Scrape into the crust and spread evenly.

3. Arrange the fruit in a pattern of circles, alternating the kiwis and the strawberries and working from the outside toward the center. Refrigerate until set, about 1 hour.

4. Melt the jelly and water in a small saucepan over low heat, cool slightly, then brush it over the entire surface of the tart.

5. Chill for several hours before serving.

6. Serve with fresh whipped cream, crème fraiche, or vanilla ice cream.

PUMPKIN PECAN TART

SERVES 6 TO 8 ✦ ACTIVE TIME: 30 MINUTES ✦ START TO FINISH: 90 MINUTES

In a twist on a traditional pumpkin pie, this tart has the pecans as the crust. The result? Delicious!

1 pecan crust
(see page 44)

1 (15-oz.) can pumpkin
puree

1 (12-oz.) can
evaporated milk

2 eggs, lightly beaten

¾ cup granulated sugar

1 teaspoon ground
cinnamon

¼ teaspoon ground
ginger

¼ teaspoon ground
allspice

½ teaspoon salt

1 cup heavy cream

2 tablespoons
confectioners' sugar

1. Preheat the oven to 350 degrees.

2. In a large bowl, stir together the pumpkin puree and evaporated milk. Add the eggs and stir to combine. Add the sugar, cinnamon, ginger, allspice, and salt and stir to combine thoroughly.

3. Pour the pumpkin mixture into the crust.

4. Put the skillet in the oven and bake for about 50 minutes, until a knife inserted near the center comes out clean. Allow to cool completely.

5. Before serving, in a large bowl, beat the heavy cream with an electric mixer until soft peaks form. Add the confectioners' sugar one tablespoon at a time until dissolved and stiff peaks form.

6. Serve the tart with the whipped cream.

CHOCOLATE FUDGE TART

SERVES 6 TO 8 ✦ ACTIVE TIME: 45 MINUTES ✦ START TO FINISH: 90 MINUTES

When you know that nothing else will do for dessert except chocolate, you'll want to make this tart. The crust is crunchy chocolate, the filling is fudgy chocolate, and you can even drizzle white chocolate over it to hit a chocolate dessert home run.

8-10 Oreo cookies, filling scraped off

½ cup (8 tablespoons) unsalted butter, divided into portions of 6 tablespoons and 2 tablespoons

10 ounces semisweet chocolate (morsels or a bar broken into pieces)

½ cup (8 tablespoons) unsalted butter, cut into pieces

2 eggs

1 cups heavy cream

½ cup sugar

1 teaspoon vanilla extract

1 pinch salt

4 ounces white chocolate morsels or pieces

1. Preheat the oven to 350 degrees.

2. In a food processor, grind the cookie pieces until they form crumbs. If you don't have a food processor, you can also put the cookie halves in a resealable plastic bag and use a rolling pin to grind them into crumbs.

3. Put the crumbs in a bowl and add 6 tablespoons of melted butter. Heat the remaining 2 tablespoons until just melted and put the butter in the cast-iron skillet to coat the bottom. Press the cookie crumb mixture into the skillet, extending the crust about half way up the sides of the skillet.

4. Bake until the crust is firm, about 10 minutes. Allow to cool.

5. In a small saucepan, combine the chocolate and butter pieces. Heat over low until both are melted and combined, stirring frequently. Set aside.

6. In a bowl, whisk together the eggs, heavy cream, sugar, vanilla, and salt. Pouring gently and steadily, add the chocolate mixture to the egg mixture, whisking as the chocolate is added. Whisk or stir to combine thoroughly.

7. Pour the chocolate mixture into the crust and shake the skillet gently to evenly distribute the liquid.

8. Put the skillet in the oven and bake for 15 to 20 minutes until the filling is set around the edges but still soft in the center. It will continue to cook when it's removed from the oven.

9. Transfer to a wire rack and allow to cool completely.

10. Before serving, put the white chocolate pieces in a microwave-safe bowl and microwave on high for 15-second intervals, stirring after each, until the chocolate is just melted. Drizzle in a decorative pattern over the tart.

WHITE CHOCOLATE TART

SERVES 6 TO 8 ✦ ACTIVE TIME: 45 MINUTES ✦ START TO FINISH: 60 MINUTES

This creamy, rich tart tastes really good in all kinds of cookie-based crusts. I made one with Pepperidge Farm Mint Milano cookies and loved the hint of mint. Almost any of the Milano flavors would work with this, so try different kinds.

8-10 Mint Milano cookies

½ cup (8 tablespoons) unsalted butter, divided into portions of 6 tablespoons and 2 tablespoons

1 (12-oz.) package white chocolate morsels

½ cup (8 tablespoons) unsalted butter, cut into pieces

2 eggs

1 cups heavy cream

½ cup sugar

1 teaspoon vanilla extract

1 pinch salt

1. Preheat the oven to 350 degrees.

2. In a food processor, grind the cookie pieces until they form crumbs. If you don't have a food processor, you can also put the cookies in a resealable plastic bag and use a rolling pin to grind them into crumbs.

3. Put the crumbs in a bowl and add 6 tablespoons of melted butter. Heat the remaining 2 tablespoons until just melted and put the butter in the cast-iron skillet to coat the bottom. Press the cookie crumb mixture into the skillet, extending the crust about half way up the sides of the skillet.

4. Bake until the crust is firm, about 10 minutes. Allow to cool.

5. In a small saucepan, combine the white chocolate morsels and butter pieces. Heat over low until both are melted and combined, stirring frequently. Set aside.

6. In a bowl, whisk together the eggs, heavy cream, sugar, vanilla, and salt. Pouring gently and steadily, add the chocolate mixture to the egg mixture, whisking as the chocolate is added. Whisk or stir to combine thoroughly.

7. Pour the chocolate mixture into the crust and shake the skillet gently to evenly distribute the liquid.

8. Put the skillet in the oven and bake for 15 to 20 minutes until the filling is set around the edges but still soft in the center. It will continue to cook when it's removed from the oven.

9. Transfer to a wire rack and allow to cool completely. Serve with almost any flavor ice cream!

CHOCOLATE CHEESECAKE TART

SERVES 6 TO 8 ✦ ACTIVE TIME: 40 MINUTES ✦ START TO FINISH: 90 MINUTES

There's something so decadent about cheesecake! It's fantastic in a cookie crust, and this one is enhanced with cocoa powder and a dash of Kahlúa liqueur.

8-10 Oreo cookies, filling scraped off

1 tablespoon unsweetened cocoa powder

2 tablespoons Kahlúa or coffee liqueur

½ cup (8 tablespoons) unsalted butter, divided into portions of 6 tablespoons and 2 tablespoons

2 (8-oz.) packages cream cheese, softened

1 cup sugar

1 tablespoon cocoa powder

½ teaspoon vanilla extract

2 eggs

1. Preheat the oven to 350 degrees.

2. In a food processor, grind the cookie pieces until they form crumbs. If you don't have a food processor, you can also put the cookie halves in a resealable plastic bag and use a rolling pin to grind them into crumbs.

3. Put the crumbs in a bowl and add the cocoa powder and Kahlúa. Stir in the 6 tablespoons of melted butter. Heat the remaining 2 tablespoons until just melted and put the butter in the cast-iron skillet to coat the bottom. Press the cookie crumb mixture into the skillet, extending the crust about half way up the sides of the skillet.

4. Bake until the crust is firm, about 10 minutes. Allow to cool. Reduce oven temperature to 325.

5. In a large bowl, mix the cream cheese with the sugar, unsweetened cocoa powder, vanilla and eggs, until thoroughly combined. Scrape the cream cheese mixture into the cooled crust.

6. Put the skillet in the oven and bake for about 40 to 60 minutes, until set.

7. Allow to cool, and refrigerate for up to 3 hours or overnight before serving.

BLACK AND BLUE GALETTE

SERVES 6 TO 8 ✦ ACTIVE TIME: 30 MINUTES ✦ START TO FINISH: 60 MINUTES

This galette—open-faced "pie"—is made with blackberries and blueberries, a beautiful combination of colors and textures. Served warm with vanilla ice cream, it's lovely to see the white ice cream melting through the crevices of the dark fruit.

1 flaky pastry crust recipe for a single crust (see page 35)

1½ cups fresh blueberries

1½ cups fresh blackberries

½ cup light brown sugar

Juice of ½ lemon (seeds removed)

3 tablespoons cornstarch

Pinch of salt

1 egg, beaten

1 tablespoon granulated sugar

Fresh berries for garnish

1. Preheat the oven to 400 degrees.

2. The crust in the skillet should be slightly larger than the bottom of the pan so that it can be folded over along the edges.

3. In a large bowl, mix the fruit with the sugar, lemon juice, cornstarch, and pinch of salt. Stir well to be sure to coat all the fruit.

4. Place the fruit in a mound in the center of the pie crust. Fold the edges of the crust over to form an edge of about 1 inch of crust. Brush the crust with the beaten egg and sprinkle it with sugar.

5. Put the skillet in the oven and bake until the filling is bubbly, which is necessary for it to thicken sufficiently, about 35 to 40 minutes.

6. Allow to cool before serving. Garnish with fresh berries.

TRIPLE BERRY GALETTE

SERVES 4 TO 6 ✦ ACTIVE TIME: 30 MINUTES ✦ START TO FINISH: 60 MINUTES

You'll soon discover why this triple berry galette is a real home run. The fruits marry perfectly, with the raspberries sweetening everything just enough. If you want to kick it up some more, consider spreading some raspberry jam on the crust before adding the fruit and baking it.

1 flaky pastry crust recipe for a single crust (see page 35)

1 cup fresh blueberries

1 cup fresh blackberries

1 cup fresh raspberries

½ cup sugar

Juice of ½ lemon (seeds removed)

3 tablespoons cornstarch

Pinch of salt

1 egg, beaten

1 tablespoon granulated sugar

1. Preheat the oven to 400 degrees.

2. The crust in the skillet should be slightly larger than the bottom of the pan so that it can be folded over along the edges.

3. In a large bowl, mix the fruit with the sugar, lemon juice, cornstarch, and pinch of salt. Stir well to be sure to coat all the fruit.

4. Place the fruit in a mound in the center of the pie crust. Fold the edges of the crust over to form an edge of about 1 inch of crust. Brush the crust with the beaten egg and sprinkle it with sugar.

5. Put the skillet in the oven and bake until the filling is bubbly, which is necessary for it to thicken sufficiently, about 35 to 40 minutes.

6. Allow to cool before serving.

SUMMER CHERRY GALETTE

SERVES 4 TO 6 ✦ ACTIVE TIME: 30 MINUTES ✦ START TO FINISH: 60 MINUTES

You can use all of the same type of cherry for this galette, or you can mix varietals. It takes some work to remove the pits from the cherries (see page 73), but it's so worth it!

1 flaky pastry crust recipe for a single crust (see page 35)

3 cups cherries, pitted and halved

½ cup light brown sugar

Juice of ½ lemon (seeds removed)

3 tablespoons cornstarch

Pinch of salt

1 egg, beaten

1 tablespoon granulated sugar

1. Preheat the oven to 400 degrees.

2. The crust in the skillet should be slightly larger than the bottom of the pan so that it can be folded over along the edges.

3. In a large bowl, mix the fruit with the sugar, lemon juice, cornstarch, and pinch of salt. Stir well to be sure to coat all the fruit.

4. Place the fruit in a mound in the center of the pie crust. Fold the edges of the crust over to form an edge of about 1 inch of crust. Brush the crust with the beaten egg and sprinkle it with sugar.

5. Put the skillet in the oven and bake until the filling is bubbly, which is necessary for it to thicken sufficiently, about 35 to 40 minutes.

6. Allow to cool before serving.

PEACH GALETTE

SERVES 6 TO 8 ✦ ACTIVE TIME: 45 MINUTES ✦ START TO FINISH: 90 MINUTES

When peaches are ripe in the mid-to-late summer, this is a super-simple way to turn them into a great dessert. Smearing some peach jam on the crust before adding the fruit will intensify the flavor of the peaches, and if you want something a little more "adult," consider adding some Amaretto liqueur to the jam instead of water.

1 flaky pastry crust recipe for a single crust (see page 35)

3 cups fresh peaches, peeled, stones removed, and sliced

½ cup sugar

Juice of ½ lemon (seeds removed)

3 tablespoons cornstarch

Pinch of salt

2 tablespoons peach jam

1 teaspoon Amaretto liqueur (optional)

1 egg, beaten

1 tablespoon granulated sugar

1. Preheat the oven to 400 degrees.

2. The crust in the skillet should be slightly larger than the bottom of the pan so that it can be folded over along the edges.

3. In a large bowl, mix the fruit with the sugar, lemon juice, cornstarch, and pinch of salt. Stir well to be sure to coat all the fruit.

4. If using the liqueur, mix it in with the jam in a small bowl before smearing the jam onto the center of the crust.

5. Place the fruit in a mound in the center of the pie crust. Fold the edges of the crust over to form an edge of about 1 inch of crust. Brush the crust with the beaten egg and sprinkle it with sugar.

6. Put the skillet in the oven and bake until the filling is bubbly, which is necessary for it to thicken sufficiently, about 35 to 40 minutes.

7. Allow to cool before serving.

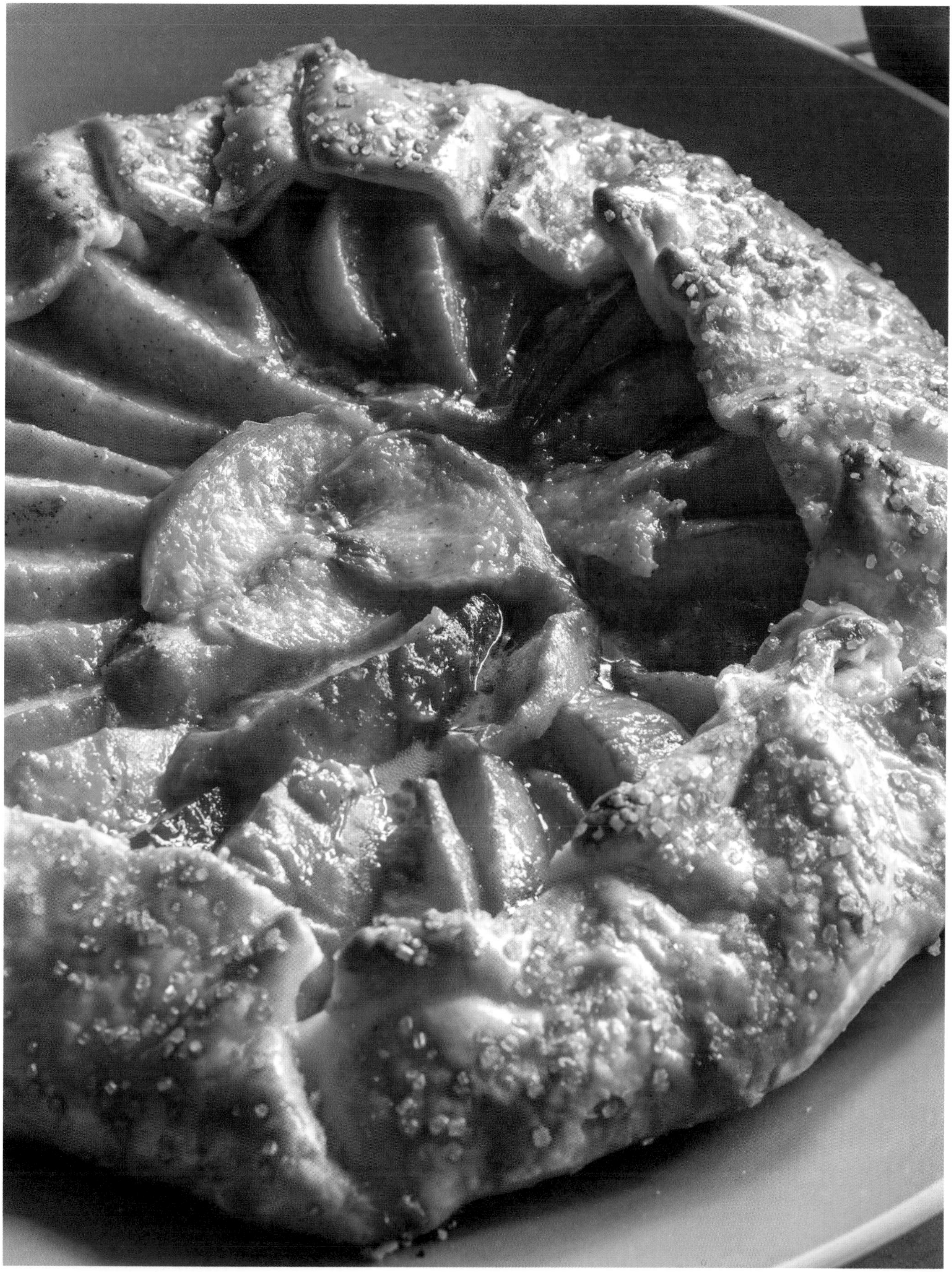

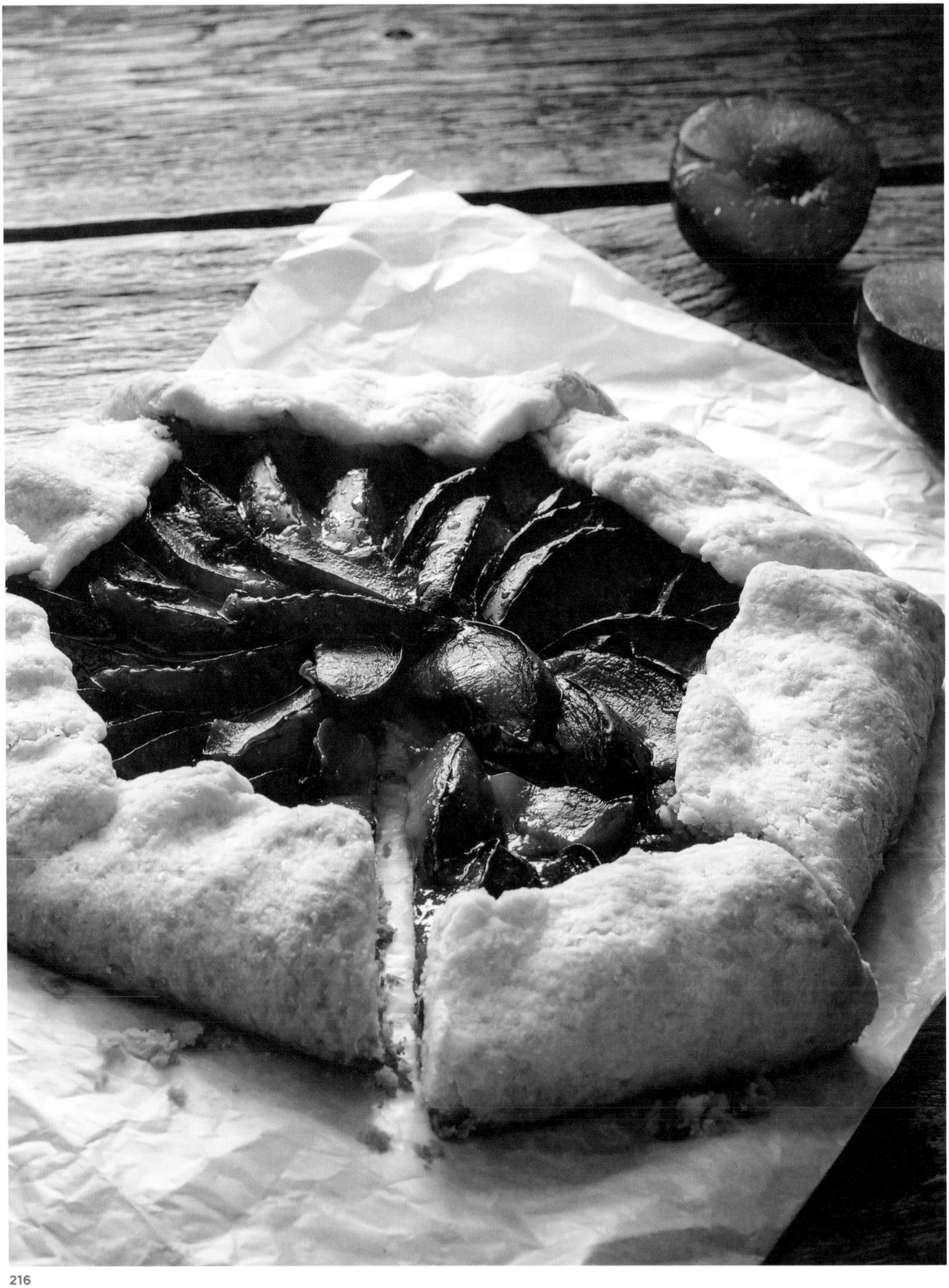

PLUM GALETTE

SERVES 4 TO 6 ✦ ACTIVE TIME: 40 MINUTES ✦ START TO FINISH: 90 MINUTES

Here's another summer fruit-laden pie that is so easy to put together and tastes great! The flavor of the plums is definitely enhanced by the jam, and the whole thing is sublime when topped with ice cream and—try this—roasted and salted pumpkin seeds (just a sprinkle).

1 flaky pastry crust recipe for a single crust (see page 35)

3 cups fresh plums, pits removed, and sliced

½ cup sugar

Juice of ½ lemon (seeds removed)

3 tablespoons cornstarch

Pinch of salt

2 tablespoons blackberry jam

1 egg, beaten

1 tablespoon granulated sugar

1. Preheat the oven to 400 degrees.

2. The crust in the skillet should be slightly larger than the bottom of the pan so that it can be folded over along the edges.

3. In a large bowl, mix the fruit with the sugar, lemon juice, cornstarch and pinch of salt. Stir well to be sure to coat all the fruit.

4. Brush or smear the jam in the center of the pie crust. Place the fruit in a mound in the center, as well. Fold the edges of the crust over to form an edge of about 1 inch of crust. Brush the crust with the beaten egg and sprinkle it with sugar.

5. Put the skillet in the oven and bake until the filling is bubbly, which is necessary for it to thicken sufficiently, about 35 to 40 minutes.

6. Allow to cool before serving.

NECTARINE-RASPBERRY GALETTE

SERVES 4 TO 6 ✦ ACTIVE TIME: 40 MINUTES ✦ START TO FINISH: 90 MINUTES

I love this flavor combination, and I love the colors, too. The best part is that it tastes even better than it looks.

1 flaky pastry crust recipe for a single crust (see page 35)

1½ cups fresh nectarines, stones removed, and sliced

1½ cups fresh raspberries

½ cup sugar

Juice of ½ lemon (seeds removed)

1 teaspoon lemon zest

3 tablespoons cornstarch

Pinch of salt

1 egg, beaten

1 tablespoon granulated sugar

1. Preheat the oven to 400 degrees.

2. The crust in the skillet should be slightly larger than the bottom of the pan so that it can be folded over along the edges.

3. In a large bowl, mix the fruit with the sugar, lemon juice, lemon zest, cornstarch, and pinch of salt. Stir well to be sure to coat all the fruit.

4. Place the fruit in a mound in the center of the pie crust. Fold the edges of the crust over to form an edge of about 1 inch of crust. Brush the crust with the beaten egg and sprinkle it with sugar.

5. Put the skillet in the oven and bake until the filling is bubbly, which is necessary for it to thicken sufficiently, about 35 to 40 minutes.

6. Allow to cool before serving.

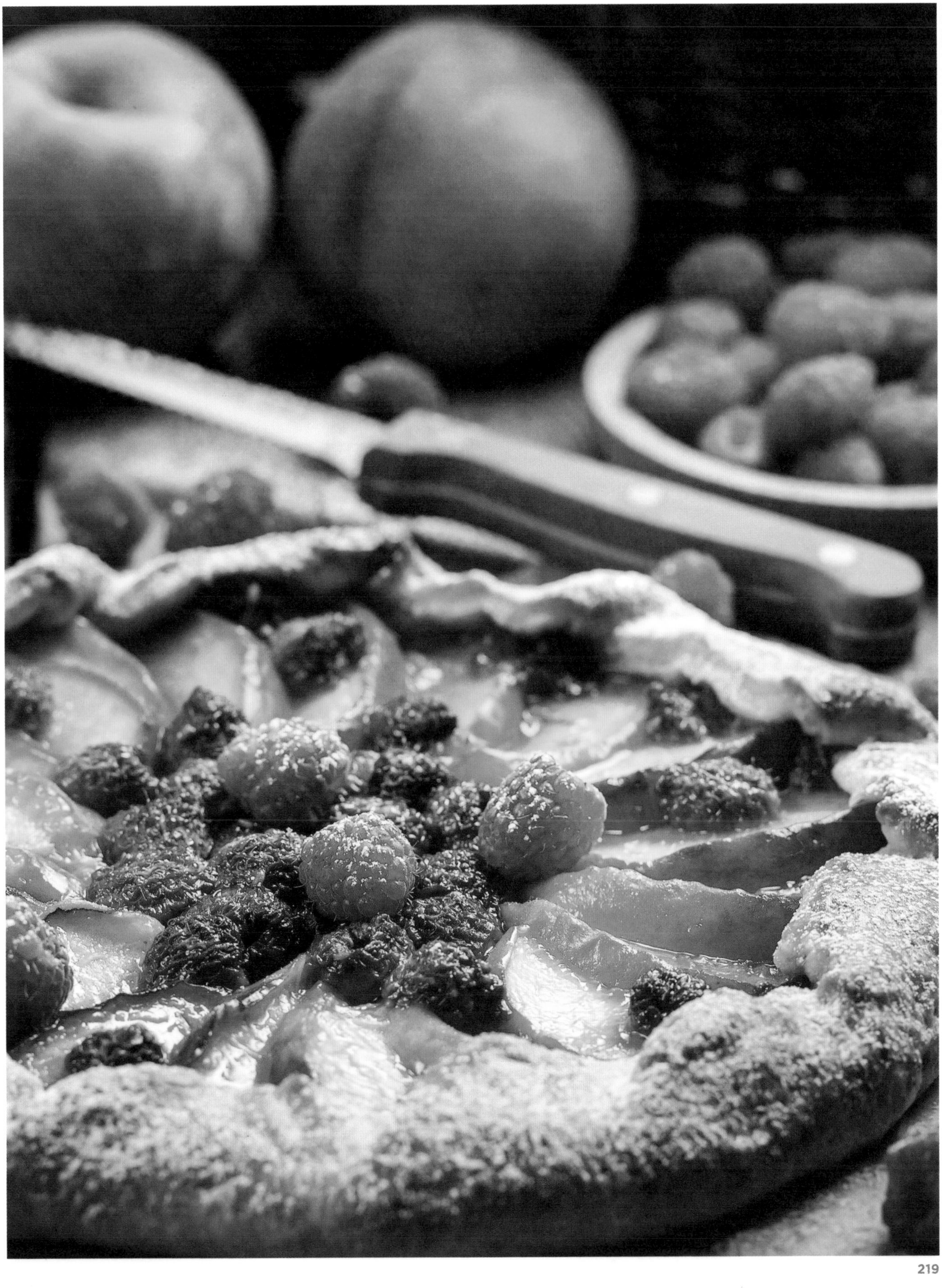

SAVORY PIES, TARTS & GALETTES

I'm a huge fan of savory pies, tarts, and galettes.
A rich, flaky pastry crust, or a layer of mashed
potatoes, makes the perfect blanket for a combination
of vegetables, meats, cheeses, or all three. These pies
are variations on pizza or flatbreads, in a way, as they
can be played with in so many ways. There are
some classic recipes in this chapter, like traditional
Shepherd's Pie, and there are some more exotic
creations, like the beet and ricotta galette, which
includes radicchio. What's the difference between
a pie, a tart, and a galette? The "pies" feature a top
crust (some have a bottom crust, some do not);
the tarts all have a signature bottom crust, but are
typically less full than a traditional pie (think quiche);
and a galette is an open-faced pie where the crust is
simply folded up around the edges and crimped.

SHEPHERD'S PIE

I'm not sure how this recipe came to be called a "pie" since it doesn't really have a crust. Instead, it has a top layer of mashed potatoes, which blankets the beef mixture underneath and helps keep it juicy while it bakes. In that sense, it works like a pie. Semantics aside, it's one of the best comfort foods you can make.

6 russet potatoes, peeled and cubed

½ teaspoon salt

½ cup (8 tablespoons) butter, cut into individual tablespoons

½ to ¾ cup milk, or ½ cup milk and ¼ cup plain yogurt

Salt and pepper to taste

1 tablespoon olive oil

½ yellow onion, chopped fine

1 pound ground beef

1 (15-oz.) can of petit pois (peas), drained, or 2 cups high-quality frozen peas

½ of a 15-oz. can of corn kernels, drained (if desired)

Salt and pepper to taste

1. Preheat the oven to 350 degrees.

2. After peeling and cubing the potatoes, give them a final rinse to get all the dirt off. Put the potato pieces in a large saucepan or pot and cover with cold water. Add the salt. Bring the water to a boil, reduce to a simmer, and cook the potatoes until soft, about 20 minutes. When they can be easily pierced with a sharp knife, they're cooked.

3. Drain the potato pieces and put them in a large bowl. Add 6 tablespoons of the butter and ½ cup of the milk and use a potato masher to make the mashed potatoes. Add additional milk or yogurt to get a creamy but not soupy consistency. Season with salt and pepper and set aside.

4. In the cast-iron skillet over medium heat, put the tablespoon of olive oil and cook the onion, stirring to just soften, about 2 minutes. Add the ground beef and break apart to cook, stirring while the meat browns. When there is just a little pinkness to the meat, drain the fat from it. Stir in the peas and, if desired, the corn kernels. Season with salt and pepper.

5. Spread the mashed potatoes over the meat and vegetables, distributing the potatoes evenly and smoothing the top. Cut the remaining 2 tablespoons of butter into slivers and dot the potatoes with them.

6. Cover with foil and bake for 30 minutes. Remove the foil and cook another 10 minutes until the potatoes are just browned.

7. Allow to cool about 5 minutes before serving.

BEEF BOURGUIGNON SHEPHERD'S PIE

SERVES 4 TO 6 ✦ ACTIVE TIME: 60 MINUTES ✦ START TO FINISH: 90 MINUTES

This is a decadent shepherd's pie, with loads of butter and cream. Celebrate its richness and don't skimp on the ingredients.

6 russet potatoes, peeled and cubed

½ teaspoon salt

½ cup (8 tablespoons) butter

¾ cup half-and-half

½ cup white cheddar cheese, shredded

Salt and pepper to taste

3 slices bacon, cut into ½-inch pieces

2 tablespoons olive oil

1½ pounds beef stew meat, cut into chunks

1 carrot, peeled, washed, and sliced

½ yellow onion, diced

½ cup sliced white mushrooms

1 tablespoon flour

1½ cups dry red wine

1 cup beef broth

1 tablespoon tomato paste

1 clove garlic, smashed

¼ teaspoon dried thyme

1 bay leaf

1. Preheat the oven to 325 degrees.

2. After peeling and cubing the potatoes, give them a final rinse to get all the dirt off. Put the potato pieces in a large saucepan or pot and cover with cold water. Add the salt. Bring the water to a boil, reduce to a simmer, and cook the potatoes until soft, about 20 minutes.

3. Drain the potato pieces and put them in a large bowl. Add 6 tablespoons of the butter and the half-and-half, and use a potato masher to make the mashed potatoes. Stir in the shredded cheese. Add additional half-and-half to get a creamy but not soupy consistency. Season with salt and pepper and set aside.

4. In the cast-iron skillet, sauté the bacon in 1 tablespoon oil for about 3 minutes, until it starts to lightly brown. Remove with a slotted spoon onto a plate lined with a paper towel.

5. Next, brown the beef pieces in the oil and bacon fat, turning to brown on all sides. Use the slotted spoon to put the beef cubes with the bacon. Put the carrots, onions, and mushrooms in the skillet and cook, stirring, until just softened, about 3 minutes. Put the beef and bacon into the skillet with the vegetables. Add the flour and continue to cook and stir another 5 minutes.

6. Stir in the wine and the broth, then the tomato paste, garlic, thyme, and bay leaf. The liquid should barely cover the meat and vegetables. Bring to a low boil over medium heat. Season with salt and pepper to taste. Cover tightly with foil and bake in the oven for 3 hours, until the meat is tender.

7. Return the skillet to the stove, remove the foil, and simmer over low heat for 5 to 10 minutes to reduce the sauce. Skim off any fat and remove the bay leaf. Increase the oven temperature to 350 degrees.

8. Spread the mashed potatoes over the beef and vegetables, distributing the potatoes evenly and smoothing the top. Cut the remaining 2 tablespoons of butter into slivers and dot the potatoes with them.

9. Cover with foil and bake for 20 minutes. Remove the foil and cook another 10 minutes until the potatoes are just browned.

INSIDE-OUT NACHO SHEPHERD'S PIE

SERVES 4 TO 6 ✦ ACTIVE TIME: 45 MINUTES ✦ START TO FINISH: 90 MINUTES

Talk about a winning one-dish meal for the family! This pot pie tastes like the best loaded nachos you've ever had, already mixed up and hot and gooey. Try it, you'll love it!

1 cornmeal crust (see page 39)

1 pound ground beef

½ yellow onion, chopped fine

2 cloves garlic, crushed

½ cup sliced black olives

¼ to ½ cup sliced jalapeño peppers (depending on how hot you like it)

½ cup corn kernels (no sugar added)

1 (15-oz.) jar diced tomatoes

1½ cups sharp cheddar cheese, shredded

1 cup (8 ounces) sour cream

Salt and pepper to taste

1 egg

1 tablespoon water

1. Preheat the oven to 350 degrees.

2. In the cast-iron skillet, brown the ground beef with the onion, sautéing until the meat is just browned and the onion is softened. Drain the fat from the meat.

3. Return the skillet to the heat and add the garlic, olives, jalapeño peppers, corn kernels, and diced tomatoes. Stir well to combine. Reduce heat to low.

4. In a bowl, stir together the cheddar cheese and the sour cream. Gently stir this into the ground meat mixture. Season with additional salt and pepper if desired. Remove from heat.

5. Top the meat mixture with the cornmeal crust. Garnish with some jalapeño slices, if desired. Beat egg with the tablespoon of water and brush over the crust.

6. Put the skillet in the oven and bake for 25 to 30 minutes until the crust is golden and the filling is bubbly.

MUSHROOM AND CHARD SHEPHERD'S PIE

SERVES 4 TO 6 ✦ ACTIVE TIME: 45 MINUTES ✦ START TO FINISH: 90 MINUTES

Here's a great recipe for a pot pie that's filling and earthy but has no meat in it. It's topped with mashed potatoes, which makes this more of a meal. Serve with a big green salad for a special brunch or light dinner.

6 russet potatoes, peeled and cubed

½ teaspoon salt

½ cup (8 tablespoons) butter, cut into individual tablespoons

½ to ¾ cup milk, or ½ cup milk and ¼ cup plain yogurt

Salt and pepper to taste

3 tablespoons butter

1 small onion, chopped fine

1 pound assorted mushrooms, rinsed and chopped, to yield approximately 3 cups

1 bunch Swiss Chard, washed and chopped (or substitute 4 cups fresh spinach leaves, stems removed)

1 tablespoon Worcestershire Sauce

Salt and pepper to taste

2 tablespoons butter, cut into slivers

1. Preheat the oven to 350 degrees.

2. After peeling and cubing the potatoes, give them a final rinse to get all the dirt off. Put the potato pieces in a large saucepan or pot and cover with cold water. Add the salt. Bring the water to a boil, reduce to a simmer, and cook the potatoes until soft, about 20 minutes. When they can be easily pierced with a sharp knife, they're cooked.

3. Drain the potato pieces and put them in a large bowl. Add 6 tablespoons of the butter and ½ cup of the milk and use a potato masher to make the mashed potatoes. Add additional milk or yogurt to get a creamy but not soupy consistency. Season with salt and pepper and set aside.

4. In the cast-iron skillet, melt the butter over medium heat and add the onions, cooking, until just softened, about 3 minutes. Add the mushrooms, the chopped stems of the chard (not the leaves), and the Worcestershire sauce. Cook over medium heat for about 3 minutes, stirring frequently, then reduce the heat to low and continue to cook for another 5 minutes or so, until the mushrooms and chard stems are soft. If the mixture seems dry, add a tablespoon of olive oil.

5. Increase the heat to medium and add the chard leaves. Cook, stirring constantly, until the leaves wilt, about 3 minutes. Remove the skillet from the heat and season with salt and pepper to taste.

6. Spread the mashed potatoes over the mushroom and chard mix, distributing the potatoes evenly and smoothing the top. Cut the remaining 2 tablespoons of butter into slivers and dot the potatoes with them.

7. Cover with foil and bake for 25 minutes. Remove the foil and cook another 10 minutes until the topping is just browned and the filling is bubbly.

LOBSTER SHEPHERD'S PIE

SERVES 4 TO 6 ✦ ACTIVE TIME: 45 MINUTES ✦ START TO FINISH: 90 MINUTES

I love this recipe because it takes "fancy" food—lobster—and makes it into something down-to-earth yet simply elegant. It makes a wonderful dinner for a date night, and it also shines as the star of Sunday brunch with family and friends.

6 russet potatoes, peeled and cubed

½ teaspoon salt

½ cup (8 tablespoons) butter, cut into individual tablespoons

½ to ¾ cup milk, or ½ cup milk and ¼ cup plain yogurt

Salt and pepper to taste

6 large leeks, white and pale-green parts only, halved lengthwise, and cut into ½-inch pieces, rinsed well

2 tablespoons flour

1 cup chicken or vegetable broth or stock

3 cups cooked lobster meat

¾ cup (6 ounces) canned peas (drained)

½ cup canned corn kernels (drained)

1 tablespoon dry sherry

Salt and pepper to taste

1. Preheat the oven to 350 degrees.

2. After peeling and cubing the potatoes, give them a final rinse to get all the dirt off. Put the potato pieces in a large saucepan or pot and cover with cold water. Add the salt. Bring the water to a boil, reduce to a simmer, and cook the potatoes until soft, about 20 minutes. When they can be easily pierced with a sharp knife, they're cooked.

3. Drain the potato pieces and put them in a large bowl. Add 6 tablespoons of the butter and ½ cup of the milk and use a potato masher to make the mashed potatoes. Add additional milk or yogurt to get a creamy but not soupy consistency. Season with salt and pepper and set aside.

4. In the cast-iron skillet over medium heat, melt the additional 2 tablespoons of butter and cook the leeks, stirring to just soften, about 2 minutes. Reduce the heat to low and cover. Cook an additional 5 to 8 minutes, stirring occasionally, until tender.

5. Stir in flour, and cook for 1 minute. Add the broth or stock, raise the heat to medium-high, and bring to a boil. Reduce heat to low, and let simmer, uncovered, for 2 minutes.

6. Stir in lobster, sherry, peas, and corn and remove from heat.

7. Spread the mashed potatoes over the lobster, distributing the potatoes evenly and smoothing the top. Cut the remaining 2 tablespoons of butter into slivers and dot the potatoes with them.

8. Cover with foil and bake for 30 minutes. Remove the foil and cook another 10 minutes until the potatoes are just browned.

9. Allow to cool slightly before serving.

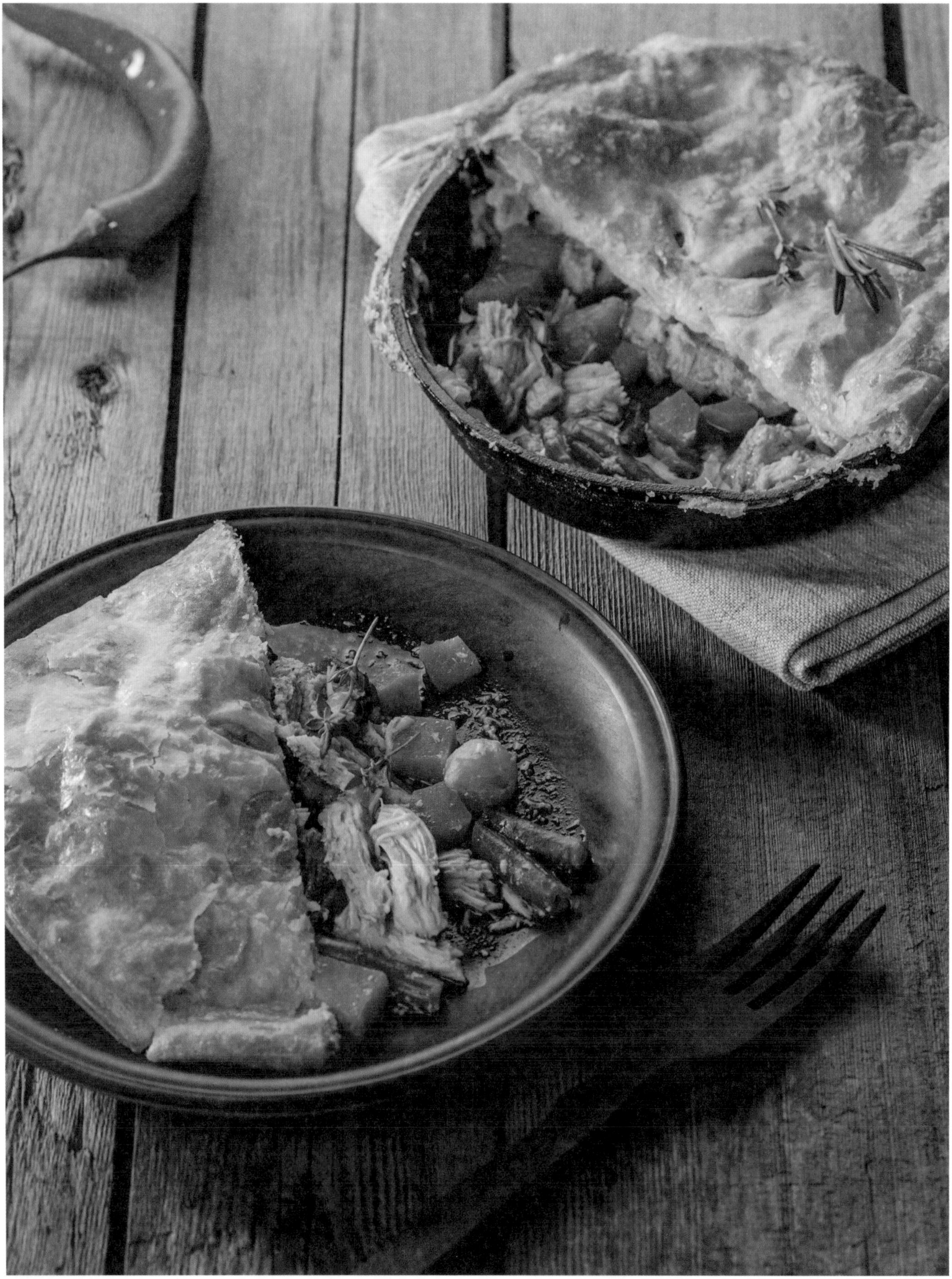

CHICKEN POT PIE

SERVES 4 TO 6 ✦ ACTIVE TIME: 60 MINUTES ✦ START TO FINISH: 2 HOURS

When you have leftover chicken, reach for this recipe. Simply prepare the chicken mixture in the skillet, top with a crust, bake, and you have a delicious and satisfying meal.

1 flaky pastry crust recipe for a single crust (see page 35)

2 tablespoons olive oil

½ yellow onion, diced

1 clove garlic, chopped

1 carrot, peeled and cut into thin rounds

2 tablespoons butter, cut into smaller slices

2 tablespoons flour

1¼ cup milk at room temperature

1½ cups cooked chicken, cut into bite-sized pieces

¾ cup frozen green bean pieces

Salt and pepper to taste

½ teaspoon cayenne (optional)

1 tablespoon half-and-half

1. Preheat the oven to 350 degrees.

2. In a small skillet (not the cast-iron skillet), heat the olive oil. Add the onion and garlic and stir, cooking, for about 2 minutes. Add the carrot slices. Reduce the heat to low and cook, covered, stirring occasionally, until the carrots start to soften and the onions caramelize, about 5 minutes. Set aside.

3. Before starting to make the white sauce, be sure the milk is at room temperature. If it's not, microwave it so that it's just warm, about 15 to 20 seconds. Have the milk ready.

4. In the cast-iron skillet, over medium heat, melt the butter. Sprinkle the flour over it and stir quickly yet gently to blend the flour in with the butter. Reduce the heat slightly so the butter doesn't burn. Stir until the butter and flour are combined, a minute or so. They will form a soft paste.

5. Add just a little of the warm milk and stir constantly to blend it in. Add more milk in small increments, working after each addition to stir it into the flour and butter mixture smoothly. Work this way until all the milk has been incorporated. Continue to stir the sauce, cooking over low heat, until it thickens, about 5 minutes.

6. Add the chicken pieces, green beans, and vegetable mixture from the other skillet. Season with salt and pepper. If you want a hint of heat, add the cayenne pepper.

7. On a lightly floured surface, roll out the crust so it will fit over the filling. Lay it gently on top, push down slightly to secure, and cut 3 or 4 slits in the middle. Brush the crust with the half-and-half.

8. Put the skillet in the oven and bake for 30 to 40 minutes, until the crust is browned and the filling is bubbly.

9. Allow to cool slightly before serving.

CHICKEN AND ARTICHOKE HEART POT PIE

SERVES 4 TO 6 ✦ ACTIVE TIME: 45 MINUTES ✦ START TO FINISH: 90 MINUTES

You could call this a pot pie Italiano, as the marinade for the artichoke hearts adds to the flavor of the dish.

1 flaky pastry crust recipe for a single crust (see page 35)

2 tablespoons olive oil from the jarred artichoke hearts

½ yellow onion, diced

1 clove garlic, chopped

1 (6-oz.) jar quartered, marinated artichoke hearts, drained and chopped

½ teaspoon oregano

½ teaspoon dried red pepper flakes (optional)

2 tablespoons butter, cut into smaller slices

2 tablespoons flour

1¼ cup milk at room temperature

1½ cups cooked chicken, cut into bite-sized pieces

1 cup frozen peas

Salt and pepper to taste

1 tablespoon half-and-half

1. Preheat the oven to 350 degrees.

2. In a small skillet (not the cast-iron skillet), heat the oil from the artichoke hearts. Add the onion and garlic and stir, cooking, for about 2 minutes. Add the artichoke hearts, oregano, and hot pepper flakes. Reduce the heat to low and cook, covered, stirring occasionally, until the vegetables soften and caramelize, about 5 minutes. Set aside.

3. Before starting to make the white sauce, be sure the milk is at room temperature. If it's not, microwave it so that it's just warm, about 15 to 20 seconds. Have the milk ready.

4. In the cast-iron skillet, over medium heat, melt the butter. Sprinkle the flour over it and stir quickly yet gently to blend the flour in with the butter. Reduce the heat slightly so the butter doesn't burn. Stir until the butter and flour are combined, a minute or so. They will form a soft paste.

5. Add just a little of the warm milk and stir constantly to blend it in. Add more milk in small increments, working after each addition to stir it into the flour and butter mixture smoothly. Work this way until all the milk has been incorporated. Continue to stir the sauce, cooking over low heat, until it thickens, about 5 minutes.

6. Add the chicken pieces, peas, and vegetable mixture from the other skillet. Season with salt and pepper.

7. On a lightly floured surface, roll out the crust so it will fit over the filling. Lay it gently on top, push down slightly to secure, and cut 3 or 4 slits in the middle. Brush the crust with the half-and-half.

8. Put the skillet in the oven and bake for 30 to 40 minutes, until the crust is browned and the filling is bubbly.

9. Allow to cool slightly before serving.

CARAMELIZED ONION TART

SERVES 4 TO 6 ✦ **ACTIVE TIME: 40 MINUTES** ✦ **START TO FINISH: 90 MINUTES**

It's simply magic how slow-cooking onions in butter renders them from pungent and sharp to mellow and almost sweet. Combine these with cheese and herbs, and you have the perfect "confit" to top a pastry crust and make a fabulous tart.

1 flaky pastry crust recipe for a single crust (see page 35)

3 cups grated Emmenthaler or genuine Swiss cheese

1 (8-oz.) package cream cheese, softened

1 tablespoon Dijon mustard

2 tablespoons butter

2-3 large yellow onions, sliced into ¼-inch slices (2-3 cups)

1 tablespoon fresh thyme

1. In a large bowl, mix the cheese, cream cheese, and mustard until well combined. Set aside.

2. In the cast-iron skillet, melt the butter and add the onions. Over medium heat, cook, stirring, until all the pieces are covered with butter and just softened, about 2 minutes. Reduce the heat to low and continue to cook, stirring occasionally, until the onions are browned and caramelized, about 1 hour. Transfer them to a bowl but keep the butter in the skillet.

3. While the onions are cooking, preheat the oven to 400 degrees.

4. On a lightly floured surface, roll out the crust so that it is just larger than the bottom of the pan and lay the pastry crust in the pan.

5. Top with the cheese/mustard mix, spreading to distribute evenly. Spread the caramelized onions over the cheese. Sprinkle with the fresh thyme.

6. Put the skillet in the oven and bake for 10 minutes at 400 degrees, then reduce the heat to 375 degrees and bake an additional 10 to 15 minutes until the crust is golden and puffy.

TURKEY AND SWEET POTATO POT PIE

SERVES 4 TO 6 ✦ ACTIVE TIME: 45 MINUTES ✦ START TO FINISH: 90 MINUTES

This is a fun pot pie to make after Thanksgiving, when there tends to be leftover turkey and sweet potatoes. Feel free to add any other vegetable leftovers into the filling, such as green beans, creamed onions, or peas. If you're inspired, add the cumin. It adds an exotic flavor and gives a nice deep yellow color to the filling.

1 flaky pastry crust recipe for a single crust (see page 35)

2 tablespoons olive oil

½ yellow onion, diced

1 clove garlic, chopped

1 small sweet potato, peeled and cut into small cubes

½ teaspoon thyme

2 tablespoons butter, cut into smaller slices

2 tablespoons flour

1¼ cup milk at room temperature

1½ cups cooked turkey, cut into bite-sized pieces

1 cup frozen peas

Salt and pepper to taste

½ teaspoon cumin (optional)

1 tablespoon half-and-half

1. Preheat the oven to 350 degrees.

2. In a small skillet (not the cast-iron skillet), heat the olive oil. Add the onion and garlic and stir, cooking, for about 2 minutes. Add the sweet potato pieces and the thyme. Reduce the heat to low and cook, covered, stirring occasionally, until the sweet potatoes start to soften and the onions caramelize, about 5 minutes. Set aside.

3. Before starting to make the white sauce, be sure the milk is at room temperature. If it's not, microwave it so that it's just warm, about 15 to 20 seconds.

4. In the cast-iron skillet, over medium heat, melt the butter. Sprinkle the flour over it and stir quickly yet gently to blend the flour in with the butter. Reduce the heat slightly so the butter doesn't burn. Stir until the butter and flour are combined, a minute or so. They will form a soft paste.

5. Add just a little of the warm milk and stir constantly to blend it in. Add more milk in small increments, working after each addition to stir it into the flour and butter mixture smoothly. Work this way until all the milk has been incorporated. Continue to stir the sauce, cooking over low heat, until it thickens, about 5 minutes.

6. Add the turkey pieces, peas, and vegetable mixture from the other skillet, along with any other leftovers you think would taste good. If needed, add some additional milk so the filling isn't too thick. Season with salt, pepper, and cumin.

7. On a lightly floured surface, roll out the crust so it will fit over the filling. Lay it gently on top, push down slightly to secure, and cut 3 or 4 slits in the middle. Brush the crust with the half-and-half.

8. Put the skillet in the oven and bake for 30 to 40 minutes, until the crust is browned and the filling is bubbly.

9. Allow to cool slightly before serving.

BEEF AND MUSHROOM POT PIE

SERVES 4 TO 6 ✦ ACTIVE TIME: 45 MINUTES ✦ START TO FINISH: 90 MINUTES

When you're looking for something to pair with a big, dry red wine and it's a chilly fall day, remember this dish. Prepare the dish early in the day, then bake about an hour before you're ready for dinner, and this pot pie will be the perfect companion to that special bottle of wine.

1 flaky pastry crust recipe for a single crust (see page 35)

3 tablespoons flour

1 teaspoon salt

1 teaspoon pepper

1 teaspoon paprika

½ cup beef pieces (stew meat)

2 tablespoons olive oil

½ yellow onion, diced

2 carrots, peeled and sliced

1 celery sticks, leaves removed, diced

1 cup mushrooms, sliced

½ cup beef broth

¾ cup stout beer

2 cloves garlic, crushed

½ teaspoon thyme

½ teaspoon rosemary

1 bay leaf

Salt and pepper to taste

1 egg

1 tablespoon water

1. Preheat the oven to 400 degrees.

2. In a large bowl, whisk together the flour, salt, pepper, and paprika. Add the beef pieces and toss to coat well. Set aside.

3. In the cast-iron skillet, heat the oil over medium-high heat. Add the floured meat pieces and stir, cooking, until just browned on the outside. Add the garlic and stir, cooking together for a minute or so. Add the onion, carrots, celery, and mushrooms, and stir to brown the vegetables, about 2 minutes. Add the broth, beer, garlic, thyme, rosemary, and bay leaf. Stir and bring to a boil, stirring occasionally, then reduce the heat to low and simmer for 10 to 12 minutes, stirring occasionally, until meat and vegetables are tender. Remove from heat and allow to cool, about 30 to 40 minutes. Remove the bay leaf. Season with additional salt and pepper, if desired.

4. On a lightly floured surface, roll out the crust so that it will just cover the meat mixture. Lay it gently on top, push down slightly to secure, and cut 4 or 5 slits in the middle. Beat egg with 1 tablespoon water and brush on the crust.

5. Bake for about 30 to 40 minutes or until crust is browned and filling is bubbly.

6. Allow to cool slightly before serving.

LAMB POT PIE

SERVES 4 TO 6 ✦ ACTIVE TIME: 45 MINUTES ✦ START TO FINISH: 90 MINUTES

An earthy, vegetable-rich lamb stew topped with a flaky, buttery crust. A great dish to end a long, cold day.

1 flaky pastry crust recipe for a single crust (see page 35)

3 tablespoons flour

1 teaspoon salt

1 teaspoon pepper

2 pounds boneless lamb meat from leg or shoulder, cut into ½-inch cubes

2 tablespoons olive oil

16 ounces (2 cups) fat-free chicken broth

1 large potato, peeled, washed, and cut into bite-sized pieces

1½ cups frozen broccoli florets

1 cup frozen peas and carrots

3 cloves garlic, finely chopped

¾ teaspoon paprika

¼ cup chopped parsley

1 egg

1 tablespoon water

1. Preheat the oven to 400 degrees.

2. In a large bowl, whisk together the flour, salt, and pepper. Add the lamb pieces and toss to coat well. Set aside.

3. In the cast-iron skillet, heat the oil over medium-high heat. Add the floured meat pieces and stir, cooking, until just browned on the outside. Add the garlic and stir, cooking together for a minute or two. Add broth, potatoes, broccoli, and peas and carrots. Bring to a boil, then reduce the heat to low and simmer for 10 minutes, stirring occasionally. Stir in the paprika and parsley, and season with additional salt and pepper to taste.

4. On a lightly floured surface, roll out the crust so that it will just cover the meat mixture. Lay it gently on top, push down slightly to secure, and cut 4 or 5 slits in the middle. Beat egg with 1 tablespoon water and brush on the crust.

5. Put the skillet in the oven and bake for 30 minutes, until the crust is browned and the filling is bubbly.

6. Allow to cool slightly before serving.

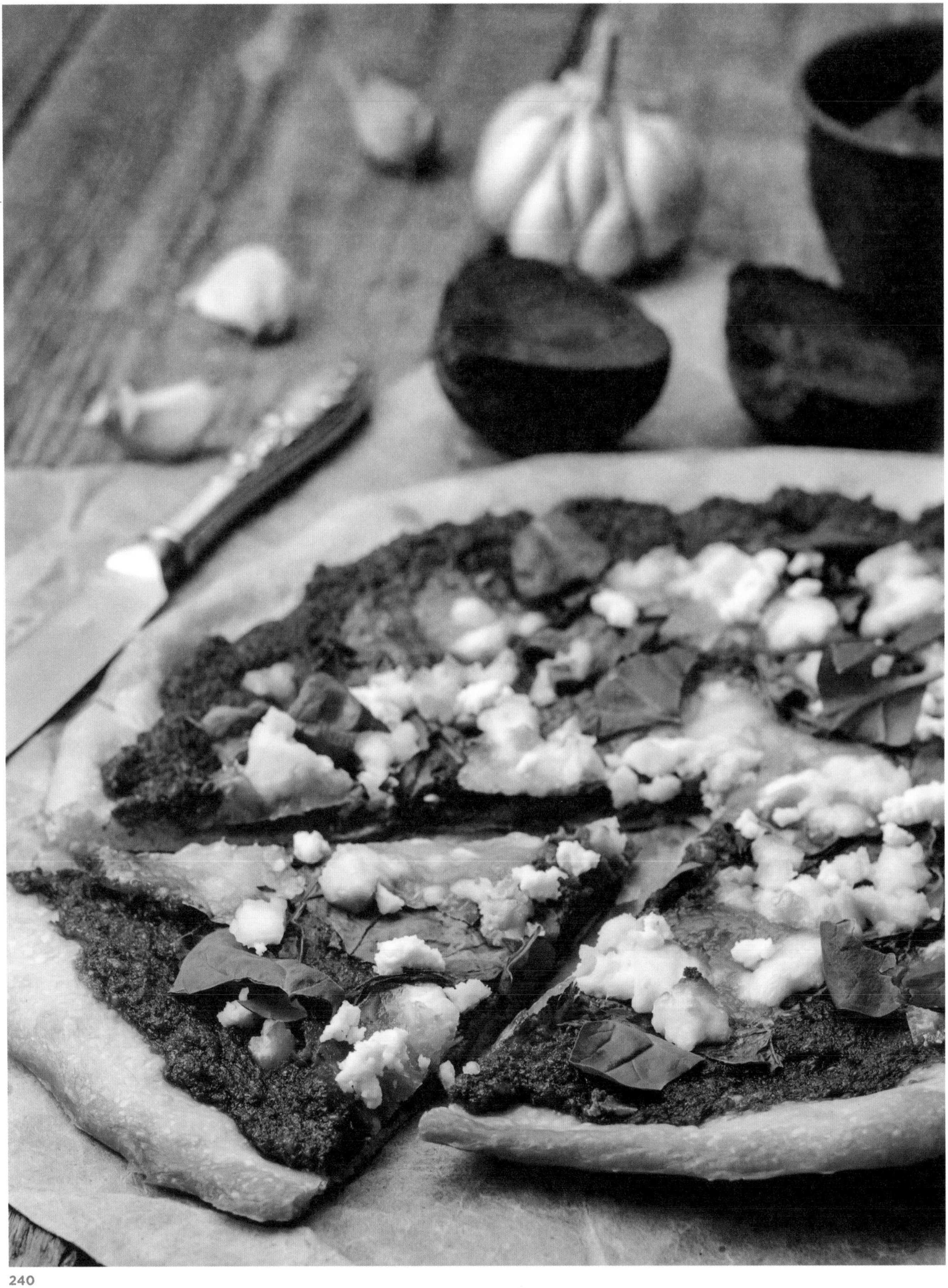

BEET AND RADICCHIO GALETTE

SERVES 4 TO 6 ✦ ACTIVE TIME: 45 MINUTES ✦ START TO FINISH: 90 MINUTES

If you want to impress some lunch guests—or yourself, for that matter—make this beautiful galette. The flavors combine beautifully, and the deep red colors are as nice to look at as they are to eat.

1 flaky pastry crust recipe for a single crust (see page 35)

1 large beet, peeled and cut into pieces

2 tablespoons olive oil, divided

2 leeks, white and light green parts only, cleaned and sliced very thin

1 head of red radicchio, sliced thin and separated so that some can be used on top

1 tablespoon balsamic vinegar

½ pound whole milk ricotta (don't substitute a lower-fat ricotta)

¼ cup grated parmesan cheese

1 egg

Salt and pepper to taste

1 tablespoon butter

1 tablespoon half-and-half

1. Preheat the oven to 400 degrees.

2. Put the beet pieces in a large piece of aluminum foil. Drizzle with the olive oil. Bake for 30 to 40 minutes until the beets are soft. Carefully remove from the oven, open the foil packet so the beets cool, and reduce the temperature to 350 degrees.

3. In a skillet other than the cast-iron, heat 1 tablespoon olive oil over medium heat, add the leeks, and cook , stirring, for about 5 minutes, until the leeks are soft and somewhat caramelized. Set ½ of the leeks aside, and add almost all the radicchio to the pan. Stir and cook over low heat, stirring occasionally, for about 8 minutes. Drizzle the balsamic over the mixture about half way through.

4. In a bowl, combine the ricotta, parmesan, and egg, mixing well. Stir in the beets and the leek/radicchio mixture, and season with salt and pepper to taste.

5. On a lightly floured surface, roll out the crust so that it is about 1 inch larger than the bottom of the pan. Melt 1 tablespoon of butter in the skillet, remove from heat, and lay the pastry crust in the pan.

6. Place the ricotta/vegetable mixture in the center. Fold the edge up and so there is about an inch of crust along the outside. Brush with half-and-half.

7. Put the skillet in the oven and bake for 25 to 30 minutes, until the crust is just golden.

8. Top with the reserved radicchio, and continue to bake for another 10 to 15 minutes.

MUSHROOM, SPINACH, AND LEEK GALETTE

SERVES 4 TO 6 ✦ ACTIVE TIME: 30 MINUTES ✦ START TO FINISH: 90 MINUTES

Caramelized leeks are even sweeter than onions, and are a great, mellow complement to the earthy mushrooms and bright spinach that top this tart.

1 flaky pastry crust recipe for a single crust (see page 35)

4 tablespoons butter

2 leeks, white and light green parts only, washed and sliced thin

1½ cups sliced mushrooms (all white mushrooms or a combination of types)

4 cups baby spinach leaves

½ cup grated parmesan cheese

1 tablespoon half-and-half

1. Preheat the oven to 375 degrees.

2. In the cast-iron skillet, melt 2 tablespoons of the butter over medium heat and add the leeks. Cook, stirring, while leeks soften, about 2 minutes. Add the remaining 2 tablespoons of butter and mushrooms, and stir to combine. Allow to cook over low heat, stirring occasionally, until mushrooms are soft and leeks are caramelized, about 10 minutes.

3. Raise the heat to medium and add the baby spinach, stirring while the leaves wilt. When wilted, remove the skillet from the heat. Transfer the vegetables to a bowl but leave the melted butter on the skillet.

4. On a lightly floured surface, roll out the crust so that it is about 1 inch larger than the bottom of the pan and lay the pastry crust in the pan.

5. Place the vegetable mixture in the center. Fold the extra crust over to form a ring around the tart, and crimp the edges gently. Sprinkle with parmesan cheese and brush the crust with the half-and-half.

6. Put the skillet in the oven and bake for 20 to 30 minutes until the crust is golden and puffy.

TOMATO, CHÈVRE, AND BASIL TART

SERVES 4 TO 6 ✦ ACTIVE TIME: 30 MINUTES ✦ START TO FINISH: 90 MINUTES

If you want to throw together an elegant and easy-to-prepare tart that celebrates summer, this is it. Use a variety of tomatoes to add color and visual appeal, as the slice sizes will be different, too.

1 flaky pastry crust recipe for a single crust (see page 35)

1½ pounds tomatoes, sliced about ¼-inch thick, seeds removed

1 tablespoon kosher salt

2 tablespoons olive oil, plus more for drizzling

1 Vidalia onion, thinly sliced

Salt and freshly ground black pepper

1 cup (8 ounces) fresh chèvre (goat cheese)

½ cup crumbled feta or grated parmesan/ romano

8-10 basil leaves, cut into threads

1. Preheat the oven to 350 degrees.

2. Put the tomato slices on a plate lined with paper towels, and sprinkle with the salt. Let the salt sit on the tomatoes for about 15 minutes, and turn the slices over.

3. In the cast-iron skillet, heat the olive oil over medium heat and add the onions. Cook, stirring, until the onions are lightly browned, about 3 minutes. Season with salt and pepper. Transfer them to a bowl but keep the oil in the skillet.

4. On a lightly floured surface, roll out the crust so that it is just larger than the bottom of the pan and lay the pastry crust in the pan.

5. Spread the onions over bottom of the crust and dot with the goat cheese. Arrange the tomato slices so that they cover the bottom. Sprinkle with the crumbled feta or parmesan/romano blend. Drizzle lightly with olive oil.

6. Put the skillet in the oven and bake at 350 degrees for 20 minutes then increase the heat to 400 degrees and bake an additional 10 minutes until top of tart is toasty

7. While tart is still warm, sprinkle with shredded basil leaves.

FIG, PROSCIUTTO, AND CAMEMBERT TART

SERVES 4 TO 6 ✦ ACTIVE TIME: 45 MINUTES ✦ START TO FINISH: 90 MINUTES

For this tart, it's important to use a baked crust, as this one doesn't need a lot of time in the oven. The figs are delicate and lose their flavor if overcooked.

1 baked crust
(see page 32)

2 tablespoons olive oil

½ onion, sliced thin

½ pound prosciutto,
cut into 1-inch slices

1 tablespoon Dijon
mustard

1 round Camembert,
at room temperature

6-8 fresh figs, stems
removed, cut in half

3 tablespoons aged
balsamic vinegar

1 tablespoon honey

1. Preheat the oven to 400 degrees.

2. In a skillet over medium heat, heat the olive oil and add the onions. Cook and stir until the onions are lightly browned, about 3 minutes. Add the prosciutto slices to the onions and cook, stirring, for an additional minute. Remove from heat.

3. Brush the Dijon mustard evenly over the bottom of the crust and top with the onion/prosciutto mix.

4. Cut the Camembert into ¼-inch thick wedges and place them decoratively over the onion mix. Next place the fig halves over the cheese. Don't overcrowd.

5. In a small bowl, whisk together the balsamic vinegar and honey. Drizzle the sauce over the tart.

6. Put the skillet in the oven and bake for 20 to 25 minutes until cheese is melted and figs are softened.

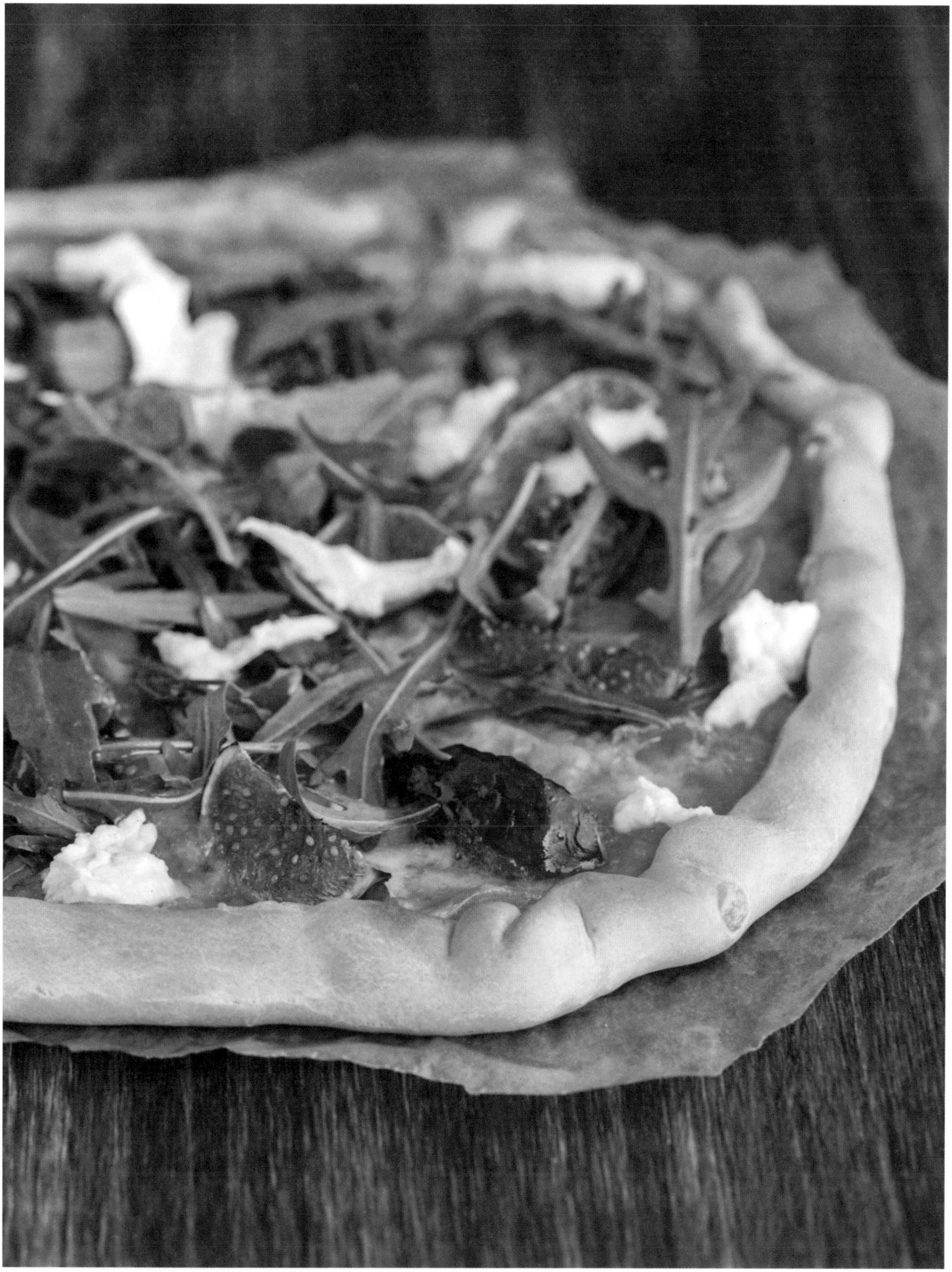

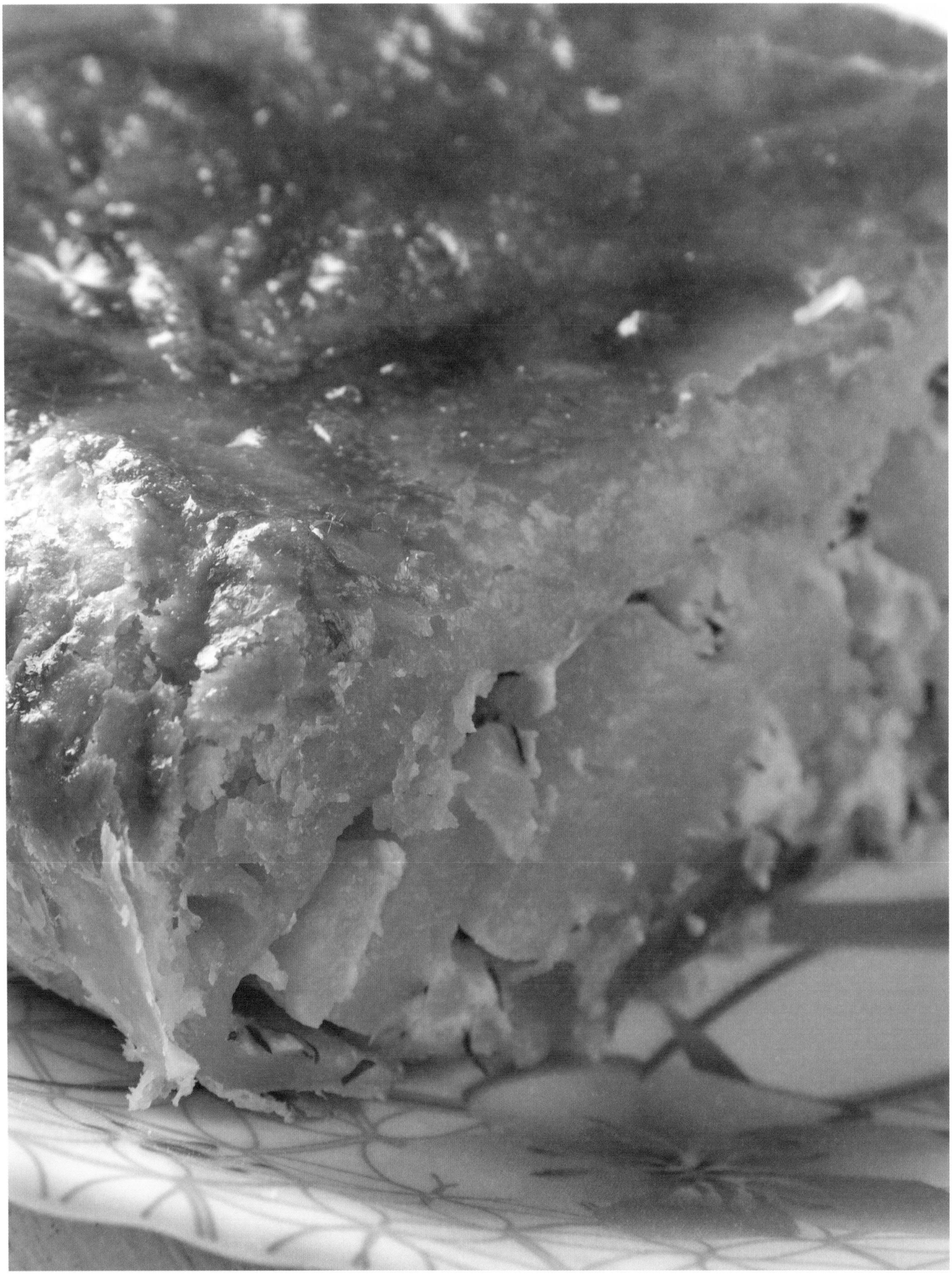

FRENCH POTATO TART

SERVES 4 TO 6 ✦ ACTIVE TIME: 45 MINUTES ✦ START TO FINISH: 2 HOURS

I refer to this as a French potato tart because of the use of crème fraîche blanketing very thin potato slices, as in a traditional gratin. What takes it over the top is baking between two crusts. This is a fantastic side dish for roast meat or vegetables.

1 flaky pastry crust recipe for a double crust (see page 35)

2 pounds Yukon Gold potatoes, peeled

1¼ cups crème fraîche

1 tablespoon kosher salt

½ teaspoon black pepper

Pinch of grated nutmeg

2 cloves garlic, crushed

2 teaspoons chopped fresh thyme

1 egg yolk

1 tablespoon half-and-half

1. Preheat the oven to 400 degrees.

2. Using a very sharp knife, a mandoline, or a spiralizer, slice the potatoes as thin as possible.

3. In a bowl, combine the crème fraîche, salt, pepper, nutmeg, garlic, and thyme. Stir to combine.

4. Add the potato slices and fold gently to cover with the crème, making sure slices are completely covered.

5. On a lightly floured surface, roll out the crust so that it is just larger than the bottom of the pan and lay the pastry crust in the pan.

6. Using your hands, start layering the potato slices in the crust, creating even, tight layers. When all the potatoes are in the crust, use a rubber spatula to scrape the cream mixture into the pie. Tap the edges of the skillet to distribute the mix evenly.

7. On a lightly floured surface, roll out the top crust and crimp the edges with the bottom crust to seal. Blend the egg yolk with the half-and-half and brush the mixture over the top crust. Cut 4 to5 slits in the middle.

8. Put the skillet in the oven and bake at 400 degrees for 15 minutes, then reduce oven temperature to 350 degrees and continue to bake for 1 hour until potatoes are tender.

9. Serve hot or at room temperature.

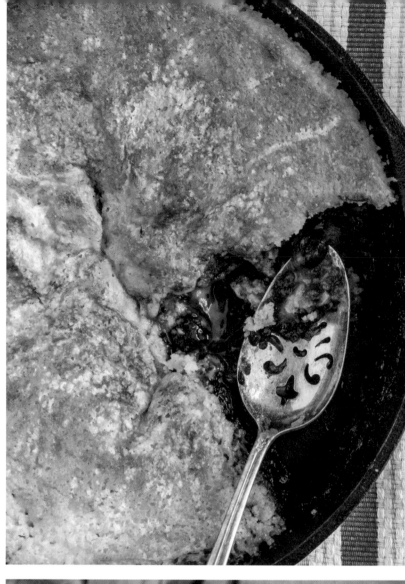

INDEX

ABOUT CIDER MILL PRESS BOOK PUBLISHERS

Good ideas ripen with time. From seed to harvest, Cider Mill Press brings fine reading, information, and entertainment together between the covers of its creatively crafted books. Our Cider Mill bears fruit twice a year, publishing a new crop of titles each spring and fall.

"Where Good Books Are Ready for Press"

Visit us on the Web at
www.cidermillpress.com
or write to us at
PO Box 454
Kennebunkport, Maine 04046

First published in 2022 by White Lion Publishing
an imprint of The Quarto Group.
The Old Brewery, 6 Blundell Street
London, N7 9BH,
United Kingdom

T (0)20 7700 6700
www.QuartoKnows.com

Text © 2022 Jess Lea-Wilson
Photography © 2022 Haarala Hamilton Photography

Printed in China

A catalogue record for this book is available from
the British Library.

ISBN 978-0-7112-6574-5
Ebook ISBN 978-0-7112-6575-2

10 9 8 7 6 5 4 3 2 1

Commissioning Editor   Melissa Hookway
Cover image   Jess Lea-Wilson
Designer   Isabel Eeles
Project editor   Charlotte Frost
Food stylist   Anna Shepherd
Publisher   Jessica Axe
Welsh translations   Angharad Griffiths
                        + Angharad Elen